Elements in Politics and Communication
edited by
Stuart Soroka
University of California

THE YOUTUBE APPARATUS

Kevin Munger
Penn State University

Shaftesbury Road, Cambridge CB2 8EA, United Kingdom

One Liberty Plaza, 20th Floor, New York, NY 10006, USA

477 Williamstown Road, Port Melbourne, VIC 3207, Australia

314–321, 3rd Floor, Plot 3, Splendor Forum, Jasola District Centre, New Delhi – 110025, India

103 Penang Road, #05–06/07, Visioncrest Commercial, Singapore 238467

Cambridge University Press is part of Cambridge University Press & Assessment, a department of the University of Cambridge.

We share the University's mission to contribute to society through the pursuit of education, learning and research at the highest international levels of excellence.

www.cambridge.org
Information on this title: www.cambridge.org/9781009486002

DOI: 10.1017/9781009359795

First published 2024

A catalogue record for this publication is available from the British Library.

ISBN 978-1-009-48600-2 Hardback
ISBN 978-1-009-35975-7 Paperback
ISSN 2633-9897 (online)
ISSN 2633-9889 (print)

The YouTube Apparatus

Elements in Politics and Communication

DOI: 10.1017/9781009359795
First published online: May 2024

Kevin Munger
Penn State University

Author for correspondence: Kevin Munger, kevinmunger@gmail.com

Abstract: The academic agenda for studying social media and politics has been somewhat haphazard. Thanks to rapid technological change, a cascade of policy-relevant crises, and sheer scale, we do not have a coherent framework for deciding what questions to ask. This Element articulates such a framework by taking existing literature from media economics and sociology and applying it reflexively, to both the academic agenda and to the specific case of politics on YouTube: the Supply and Demand Framework. The key mechanism, traced over the past century, is the technology of audience measurement. The YouTube audience comes pre-rationalized in the form of Likes, Views and Comments, and is thus unavoidable for all actors involved. The phenomenon of "radicalization" is best understood as a consequence of accelerated feedback between audiences and creators, radicalizing each other. I use fifteen years of supply and demand data from YouTube to demonstrate how different types of producers respond more or less to this feedback, which in turn structures the ideological distribution of content consumed on the platform. This title is also available as Open Access on Cambridge Core.

Keywords: YouTube, supply and demand, quantitative description, academic agenda-setting, YouTube is other people

ISBNs: 9781009486002 (HB), 9781009359757 (PB), 9781009359795 (OC)
ISSNs: 2633-9897 (online), 2633-9889 (print)

Contents

1 Foreword

This Element is structured as an extended essay intended to be read sequentially but divided into sections that can be read separately. The first three sections clear the ground for the analysis that follows, and are necessary to justify my approach. The next four sections introduce my Supply and Demand Framework and draw connections between relevant literatures and the distinct systems which are part of what I call the YouTube Apparatus. The following section presents my empirical evidence, the final section my suggestions for future research.

My substantive thesis is that demand creates its own supply: The automatically measured and quantified audience causes YouTube creators to adapt their offerings. My empirical strategy is to classify a large sample of political YouTube channels as either affiliated with some larger media entity or as independent – the latter are the classic "YouTube creators," whose personalistic style and intense audience cultivation engenders para-social relationships with their viewers. With over fifteen years of data, I demonstrate that this distinction between affiliated channels and independent YouTubers results in significant system-level differences in a variety of platform-defined audience metrics.

My meta-scientific thesis, however, is that dry science-y prose like the preceding paragraph is the final but perhaps least important step in the study of social media. Setting the academic agenda is paramount; our answers can only be as good as our questions. So I begin by applying theories of media agenda setting reflexively, in order to understand why such disproportionate effort has been applied to the relatively narrow question of the effect of the YouTube recommendation algorithm on viewers' political beliefs.

It is not yet possible to bring comprehensive data to bear on this meta-scientific question. My hope is that beginning to theorize about setting the academic agenda will inspire more systematic investigation. But this area of inquiry is distinct from our normal science work: When we study ourselves, we immediately change ourselves. So for this process to yield benefits in our study of others, we need some sense of our goals, of what we are trying to achieve. It is both untenable and irresponsible to maintain a distinction between positive and normative meta-science.

My goal, then, is to move the academic agenda for studying social media in the direction of my Supply and Demand Framework. Compared to the status quo, this means more attention to the production of content, to the forces that shape the way in which people decide to post. More broadly, my goal is to align the study of social media with *what social media is*. This is why I study

YouTube, the platform for which the ratio of academic attention to social and political importance seems to me to be the most out of whack. Methodologically, I eschew causal inference in favor of pure quantitative description, the most important tool for understanding *what* and *how much* social media is.

As I argue in the final section, another underappreciated method for setting the academic agenda is poetry. The creation and circulation of resonant metaphors carves up the conceptual space in ways that imply certain research questions (and therefore also the answers generated by rigorous normal science). So while the reader may or may not find compelling the poetic flourishes throughout, I hope you understand why I feel they are necessary.

To restate my substantive conclusion in the words of media theorist Vilém Flusser: "Those who participate actively in the production of information … are themselves being programmed by the mass-media meat choppers for information production."

Or more simply, YouTubers are not "Creators" but *Creations*. Audiences, rationalized by the platform, and the vloggers who upload the videos those audiences consumer are not separable either theoretically or empirically. Together, they make up the YouTube Apparatus.

2 Setting the Academic Agenda

To date, research on social media and politics has been somewhat haphazard. Because of the speed of technological change, the sheer scale of our object of inquiry, the necessity of disciplinary and methodological pluralism, and a cascade of policy-relevant crises, our epistemic community is not yet mature. Perhaps this is for the best; some "mature" areas of social science are facing a variety of crises grappling with methodological revolutions, and the creation of new subfields is an integral part of the scientific process.

This generally congenial anarchy has some drawbacks, however. The chain of academic knowledge production is only as strong as its weakest link, and our first link is the weakest. There is a lack of rigor allocated to the selection of *questions* we ask.

There is a meta-irony here. In this Element, I will argue in favor of a Supply and Demand Framework for studying social media, building on the literature in media economics and how these models have understood previous media-technological regimes. I will advocate for the use of these models in the study of both the contemporary media environment and the "media systems" at the heart of a variety of social media platforms.

And I will also, in passing, use these models *reflexively* to explain how our sociotechnical environment has affected the process by which the academic agenda is set.

For example, the theory of "media storms" developed in Boydstun (2013) falls under what I call the "industrial organization" of news media. This means centering the *physical* aspect of the logistical supply chain required for news production, rather than abstracting away from temporality and distance. This approach yields the insight that news is unexpectedly "sticky": The fixed costs involved in paying for reporters' and producers' travel reduce the speed at which news organizations can switch from one story to another. Furthermore, the physical proximity of news teams to a story makes it more likely that they uncover unexpected aspects or follow-ups to that story. Boydstun, Hardy, and Walgrave (2014) argues that "imitation plays a big role in determining the duration of a storm; until another hot item hits, news outlets are loathe to be the first to drop coverage of an ongoing storm, even if the event or issue itself has run its course" (p513).

Like all models, this model should not be trivially applied beyond the context it was developed to explain. To understand "academic storms," we must use our substantive (qualitative and quantitative) knowledge to adjust the parameters Boydstun identifies as important. Two such parameters strike me. The audience for academic journal articles, and the physical and temporal reality confronted by the authors of journal articles, is different than that of general news media and reporters, respectively. The psychological aspect of the drive for imitation, a key part of human nature, remains the same across contexts.

A related example comes from Usher (2014), an ethnographic investigation of the status games within the *New York Times*. I call this work "economic sociology," a crucial refinement of the lived experience of a class of news producers that provides a more realistic picture of the incentives and pressures *they perceive* as most important. She describes the status competition among veteran journalists not to maximize online news sharing or some other immediately relevant economic metric, but to get their bylines on the front page of the print edition. While the baseline approach from Economics would be to proceed with standard assumptions about the agents' utility functions, this more sociological approach begins by actually understanding the day-to-day experience of those actors – undeniably a more accurate micro-foundation, but one which is necessarily more difficult to generalize from.

Without putting too fine a point on it, we likely all appreciate the distance between the nominal goals of academics to generate knowledge or to inform policy debates and the daily experience of academics embedded in our own kind of status competition.

Matt Hindman's work provides a final example, as well as quantitative models that directly inspire some of the analysis in this Element. Hindman (2008) and Hindman (2018) both argue against two of the fundamental myths of contemporary political communication: that the lack of physical frictions from previous media regimes means that the online media landscape is more *democratic* and that it can *change overnight*.

Rather than analyzing individual actors' preferences, incentives, and information flows, Hindman's macro-level approach makes claims about the system as a whole. In a memorable example, Hindman (2018) argues that Trump-era Federal Communications Commissioner Ajit Pai is incorrect that the contemporary digital news environment requires fewer regulations because "we get news and analysis throughout the day from countless national and local websites, podcasts and social media outlets": "it is flatly not true that there are 'countless' local digital news outlets. We know, *because we counted them*" (p131). Hindman's analysis also demonstrates that the forces of concentration in digital media outweigh the forces of democratization, and that advantages to scale tend to *compound* over time, further reinforcing the advantage of established incumbents. Although the technical capacity to broadcast information has indeed been spread more evenly by digital media, the reality of *attention* as the scarce resource has tended to dominate.

Within academic research, everyone is now technically able to share their research freely and to anyone in the world. Consonant with Hindman's theory, however, the use of Twitter to share published research in Political Science tends to reinforce rather than undercut existing status hierarchies (Bisbee, Larson, and Munger, 2022). And despite the revolutionary potential of online models for academic publishing, peer review at top journals is grinding to a halt as their gatekeeping function has become even more entrenched.

Although I have laid out the applications of these models and the parameters I believe have shifted between the news media and scholarship, I expect that my readers bring a wealth of their own knowledge to this area of meta-scientific inquiry. I have ideas about how the academic agenda is set now and how it might be set differently, some of which I lay out in the following section.

My primary goal, however, is to *put the question of academic agenda setting on the academic agenda*, to argue that this is an important link in the chain of knowledge creation, and to suggest the Supply and Demand Framework as a useful first step.

I am far from the first to make such a claim. Indeed, I draw heavily on Bennett and Iyengar (2008), a high-profile and influential effort to reset the academic agenda in light of "the changing foundations of political communication." They argue that paradigms developed by the pioneers of the discipline may no longer be relevant, specifically citing "agenda setting" as a broadcast-era theory that has outlived its relevance.

Much of the ensuing debate rested on their provocative title claim of a return to the era of "minimal effects," but this is not my focus. Ironically, debating the validity of old paradigms merely serves to reinforce their relevance: Agenda setting, after all, tells us that the media (here, academic journal articles) is effective at telling us *what to think about.*

So I agree with Bennett and Iyengar (2008) that the shadow of Theory in a dynamic world can obscure social science practice. They predicted "another time of unsettled findings accompanied by the risk of undertheorized sociotechnological conditions" (p708), a prediction which I believe has been borne out. I will pick up on several trends they identify as newly important in the current media environment, an environment that has changed faster and more dramatically than most scholars (and indeed, most humans) thought possible.

In the broadest possible strokes, the "broadcast paradigm" is primarily focused on the following relationship:

Producer → Media → Consumer

There are a fantastic array of refinements that have made this a fruitful area of research, but this relationship is the core of the previous era.

Bennett and Iyengar (2008) argue that the coming era, our era, will be primarily characterized by a rise in the importance of the *exact inverse* of this relationship:

Consumer → Feedback → Producer

and the following prediction by Chaffee and Metzger (2001) seems even more prescient than it did in 2008: "The key problem for agenda setting theory will change from what issues the media tell people to think about to what issues people tell the media they want to think about" (p375).

Of course, both of these phenomena exist, the relationship between audience and creators is bidirectional, reciprocally causal, and embedded in overlapping sociotechnical contexts. I focus on how this relationship develops on each of the social media platforms that have come to dominate online communication; that is, this Element centers the "technology that shapes consumption, distribution, and content production" (p712). Or, as I call it, the Supply and Demand Framework.

The central dynamic of my framework is circular, so it is difficult to fully capture in the linear medium of text or with the unidirectional causality approaches currently in vogue in much of social science. As much as I love writing and causal inference, our objects of study do not always contort themselves into ideal forms for our preferred models and paradigms. And I believe that both the general media ecosystem and the local environments on a given platform are best understood through my Supply and Demand Framework. This Element provides a detailed application of the Framework to the study of YouTube Politics, one of the most important yet under-studied components of the contemporary US media environment.

As a political scientist, my primary (but far from exclusive) interest is in the effect of YouTube on the beliefs of citizens who consume YouTube videos and who might vote based on the information they receive in doing so. Taking this larger question of "What does YouTube do to American Politics?" as largely fixed, both by disciplinary convention and self-evident importance to a citizen of the United States, my framework can be used to divide up this daunting task into more manageable, empirical study-sized chunks. This is what I mean by "setting the academic agenda."

My hope is that this framework will allow scholars to situate and synthesize existing approaches to studying social media. That is, I do not see this framework as invalidating any existing research, but rather enhancing its value by suggesting pathways of knowledge circulation. In particular, I argue that mapping out all of the potential inputs to the YouTube system is helpful in keeping track of what scholars do and do not yet know, and therefore to decide what they should study next.

This cannot be a deterministic process, and different scholars can of course contribute in different ways based on their preexisting interests and competencies. I will, however, propose a heuristic for researchers deciding on a specific research question:

Heuristic: Study what is under-studied.

This sounds tautological, but it requires keeping two parameters in mind. First, we should spend more of our time studying what is more important; I'm not arguing for an equal distribution of scholarly attention across every conceivable area of inquiry. Note also that this parameter is intrinsically normative: While I will propose some baseline metrics for importance, this parameter is ultimately determined by our collective or respective *goals*.

Second, we need to invest in some empirical measures of how we are *currently* distributing our scholarly attention. Even if we know how much a given topic should be studied, in order to know whether we should study it more or less, we need to know what we're doing now.

Like all human endeavor, this process is not perfectible: Some kind of overreaction to thermostatic correction is inevitable, and the social phenomena we study are far from static. Worse, these two processes are not independent: Part of the knowledge generated by research is precisely about the importance of a given topic. The edge case of this problem are the "unknown unknowns": When the world produces some novel phenomenon, we start out knowing nothing about it and thus cannot deliberate over its importance or decide to allocate our time to studying it.

As a scholar of digital media for nearly a decade, this very first link in the chain of knowledge production has frequently posed a challenge. My long-standing habits of trawling obscure corners of the internet (now fully rationalized as "exploratory research") reveal some new platform, trend, or ideological current that might be important. How can I check my intuitions – that is, how can I make this case to myself?

More importantly for the academic environment, how can I convince funders and peer reviewers that this new phenomenon is important? In 2015, my first research on Twitter faced significant headwinds from my peers, who did not see why online behavior was important for understanding contemporary politics. Sure, Twitter was important as a tool for protesters and activists spreading tactical information; the Arab Spring and the wave of anti-capitalists protests in the early 2010s had put that topic firmly on the academic agenda. But why, as the old saw goes, should we care about what anyone had for lunch?

3 There Is Something Wrong on the Internet

Despite an explosion of academic interest in digital media over the past decade, the topic is still *dramatically* understudied. If you believe, like I do, that we are living through a media-technological upheaval rivaled only by that occasioned by the printing press, it is difficult to imagine studying anything else.

But even a skeptical, hard-nosed social scientist, beginning with the Aristotelian premise that humans *are* what we *do*, is forced to recognize that digital media production and consumption makes up an increasingly large percentage of the average human's waking hours.

Allen et al. (2020) provides one of the most comprehensive pictures of total media consumption in the United States to date; they find that as of 2018, the average American spends 460 minutes a day (7.5 hours) consuming media. Among the youngest age group, eighteen to twenty-four years old, this number is just under six hours a day (351 minutes); 207 of those minutes are spent on a mobile device, and another fifty-four minutes on a desktop computer.

Unfortunately for traditional methods for measuring media consumption, the diversity of options makes survey enumeration useless for all but the broadest categories. Someone might be able to tell you that they spent fifteen minutes on TikTok, but asking them "which videos" or even "which creators" they watched is not a robust measurement strategy.

The situation on the supply side of digital media is if anything more dire: The number of people empowered to *produce* media has exploded, rendering quantitative comparison absurd. More hours of video media are recorded and uploaded to YouTube and TikTok in a day than were created in the world in a decade during heyday of the postwar broadcast media.

This deluge of content makes the task of setting the academic agenda difficult. Where do we even begin!?

One entry point for many scholars is simply to use our intuitions, developed from our personal experience with digital media. This was a reasonable strategy with broadcast media; Walter Cronkite was in fact broadly representative of the political media diet of the country as a whole.

The rise of the internet changed everything. It allows production and consumption at a scale far beyond mass media, rendering it impossible for an individual to know what everyone else is up to simply by being an avid and broad consumer of political media. This in turn makes the nonrepresentativeness of social scientists' media diets a problem for our understanding of important trends in the media sphere.

We know that social scientists are intensely nonrepresentative of the populations that we study. Despite considerable progress over the previous decades, this nonrepresentativeness persists for demographic groups other than white American men. This legacy of discrimination persists in the inherited boundaries of the canonical areas of study within media and communication, particularly when it comes to the boundary of "political" media (Freelon, Malmer, and Pruden, 2023).

Even if these biases were fully rectified, we would still face a fundamental problem: *By construction*, political science professors are much better educated and more interested in politics, and we have the capacity to consume massive amounts of political media. There is widespread recognition that we need to remind ourselves of these baseline facts – the central insight of perhaps the most important book about American public opinion (Converse, 1964) is that most people simply don't care about politics–but it is all too easy to rely on the intuitions of our colleagues, peer reviewers, and funders.

We are deeply, professionally invested in the technologies of writing, deliberation, and scientific debate. As the sociologist of science Bruno Latour pointed out, if we simply observe the actions that scientists take rather than accepting our stated higher purpose, it becomes clear that our job is to *read and write papers* (Latour and Woolgar, 2013). Boundary-pushing weirdos in media studies departments aside, we are not primarily invested in watching and recording videos.

In fact, through both introspection and discussion with colleagues, it is clear that many academics actively can't stand to consume information in video format; we'd much rather read it. The average person, unfortunately for the academic agenda, is the exact opposite: They dislike reading, and have abandoned text-based digital media like blogs as soon as possible. Twitter, despite being perhaps the best-studied social media platform, has never been used by more than 25 percent of US adults. Many professors have noticed a steep decline in the writing ability of incoming undergrads. People who have been teaching for forty years noticed a slight degradation over the decades, but the past ten and especially five years have seen a collapse.

The academic agenda has yet to adapt to the reality that the majority of time spent on social media is spent on non-textual platforms. For a variety of reasons, some legitimate others merely omphalocentric, we spend far too much time studying Facebook and especially Twitter.

The media is how we learn about the world outside of our own experience (Mutz, 1998). We rely on the media to tell us about important trends in other realms of social life. The problem is that academics and media professionals inhabit a mutually constituted and reinforcing echo chamber.

The term "echo chamber" here is not used casually. This *phrase* has been disproportionately effective in setting the academic agenda for studying social media, especially in the first decade after its birth. "Echo chamber" simply rings true, a fundamentally *poetic* achievement that is upstream of quantitative research. One of the ways the academic agenda is set, then, is through **resonant metaphors**; pun on "echo chamber" intended and not at all incidental. For example, Simon and Camargo (2023) investigate the usage and implications of the "infodemic" metaphor that emerged to describe misinformation around COVID-19.

Considerable energy has been spent investigating the phenomenon of echo chambers. My summary of the literature is that it finds that they don't exist – except among users in specialized (partisan or professional) networks.

What threshold of diversity of media diet would be sufficient to falsify the existence of "echo chambers?" No one denies that online media diets are highly skewed. But the threshold can't just be greater than 50 percent congruent information; that's trivial given any amount of media choice. For now, let's consider a definition based on the offline baseline: Online echo chambers exist if the online news consumers get a higher percentage of their news from congruent sources than do offline news consumers.

Using this conception, the most comprehensive peer-reviewed paper on the topic, Guess (2021) concludes that "if 'echo chambers' exist, they are a reality for relatively few people who may nonetheless wield disproportionate influence and visibility in society" (p1007). Writing in a Knight Foundation White paper, Guess and co-authors did not feel the need to be quite so circumspect: "public debate about news consumption has become trapped in an echo chamber about echo chambers that resists corrections from more rigorous evidence" (p15).

This realization is unpleasant for diehard Popperians who still believe that science progresses through falsification, that there could exist a "critical experiment" that would convince social scientists to stop saying the words "echo chamber." The meta-scientific approach I advocate here requires that we understand science as to a significant degree a *social* process. We started saying "echo chamber" for nonquantitative reasons; it is therefore implausible to expect quantitative evidence to convince us to stop saying "echo chamber." Falsification simply does not describe the process of social science (Feyerabend, 1975).

In addition to resonant metaphors, another important way in which the academic agenda is set is the sudden eruption of some social media phenomenon from outside of academics' direct experience into the public consciousness; in short, through **media panics**.

The most dramatic example is of course the avalanche of academic research on online mis/disinformation or "Fake News" in the wake of the 2016 US Presidential Election. This makes sense; democratic societies around the world continue to grapple with this novel epistemic problem, one that threatens the foundations of the liberal reason at the heart of our political system.

We now recognize the magnitude and scope of the problem posed by online misinformation, tragically reinforced by the immediate physical harm caused by COVID-19 vaccine denialism. But we might productively ask why it took the shock electoral victory of Donald Trump to get the topic pride of place on the academic agenda. Though Trump was undoubtedly an innovator in the form, it is difficult to imagine that US-based academics would be spending quite as much time studying misinformation in the Global South today if Hillary Clinton had won a few hundred thousand more votes in Michigan, Pennsylvania, and Wisconsin.

Online misinformation, and even anti-vaccine narratives, were certainly topics of research before 2016 (Bode and Vraga, 2015; Cook, Ecker, and Lewandowsky, 2015; Garrett and Weeks, 2013; Kata, 2010, 2012). They were thus "known unknowns": We knew that these phenomena *existed*, and that we didn't yet know everything about them. But there wasn't exactly a special issue of *Science* about vaccine denialism published before 2020.

Among phenomena on digital media, however, media panics more often involve the discovery of "unknown unknowns." Again, digital media is so vast and so dynamic that it is impossible for personal experience to keep up. So these media panics serve a valuable purpose, of making academics aware of these potentially important phenomena.

But this method for setting the academic agenda has significant flaws. The same dynamics that Boydstun, Usher, and Hindman describe apply to the academic study of the current media regime. I will provide two examples from the case of YouTube.

3.1 YouTube, the Great Radicalizer

On March 10, 2018, the *New York Times* published an op-ed column with this title (Tufekci, 2018). The author, sociologist Zeynep Tufecki, describes her experience using YouTube to watch videos of Donald Trump rallies, only to notice "something peculiar. YouTube started to recommend and 'autoplay' videos for me that featured white supremacist rants, Holocaust denials and other disturbing content."

She then created fresh accounts, and started watching videos about leftist politics, running and diets.

> The same basic pattern emerged. Videos about vegetarianism led to videos about veganism. Videos about jogging led to videos about running ultramarathons. … It seems as if you are never 'hard core' enough for YouTube's recommendation algorithm. It promotes, recommends and disseminates videos in a manner that appears to constantly up the stakes. Given its billion or so users, YouTube may be one of the most powerful radicalizing instruments of the 21st century.

The anecdotal account and necessarily (given the mass audience) underspecified research design is thus far couched in the language of uncertainty, but Tufecki concludes that "YouTube leads viewers down a rabbit hole of extremism, while Google racks up the ad sales."

This oped has been cited 371 times in the past four years, per Google Scholar, and has been incredibly influential in how academics, politicians, and citizens have approached the topic of politics on YouTube. What was formerly an "unknown unknown" due to the anti-video bias of journalists and academics was thrust onto the academic agenda.

This Rumsfeldian "(un)known (un)knowns" linguistic construction has more scholarly analogues, but resonant metaphors win the day. The binary distinction is of course inaccurate; for any given phenomenon, there is a continuum of awareness among citizens, scholars, and politicians. For example, O'Callaghan et al. (2015) posits and investigates the phenomenon of "YouTube rabbit holes" for right-wing extremist content, driven by the recommendation algorithm. This paper has been cited only 184 times – but only 22 of those citations date to before the publication of Tufecki's oped.

3.2 "There Is Something Wrong on the Internet"

A few months earlier, on November 7, 2017, writer and artist James Bridle published a blog post with this title (Bridle, 2017). The central, incendiary claim is that "Someone or something or some combination of people and things is using YouTube to systematically frighten, traumatise, and abuse children, automatically and at scale."

Bridle documents the existence of millions of videos then hosted on YouTube that clearly aim at – and achieve – viewership among young children, toddlers, and even infants. These videos range from re-uploads of popular broadcast children's content to mobs of amateurs creating genres that have proven popular. To illustrate, the highest-paid YouTube channel in 2018 was "Ryan ToysReview" (revenue: $22 million). Ryan was a seven-year-old who plays with toys. The channel's most popular video has been viewed over one billion times. Ryan has hundreds of copycat channels, which all broadly operate in the genre of "unboxing videos."

Beyond the absurd and inane style inherent to children's television, there are far more troubling videos that Bridle documents. Thousands of "disturbing Peppa Pig videos, which tend towards extreme violence and fear, with Peppa eating her father or drinking bleach." In general, a formula seems to have been hit upon: "Familiar characters, nursery tropes, keyword salad, full automation, violence, and the very stuff of kids' worst dreams. … Channel after channel after channel of similar content, churned out at the rate of hundreds of new videos every week. Industrialised nightmare production."

In this case, YouTube's response was swift and heavy-handed. There had been growing awareness of something unsavory going on with children's You-Tube through 2017, and Bridle's article was pivotal in mainstreaming of what has been termed "Elsagate" due to the prominence of that particular cartoon character in these videos. Within weeks, the specific channels and videos cited by Bridle were removed, as were a large (if unknown) number of others. His blog post has been cited sixty-seven times, only a few of these by scholars of political communication.

The "YouTube Rabbit Hole" and "Elsagate" are both powerful metaphors describing attention-grabbing phenomena. The latter was identified a few months earlier than the former, which ultimately came to dominate the academic and public agenda. Why?

Part of advancing the positive study of academic agenda setting requires addressing the normative question of what *should* scholars do with these media panics? We are the ones deciding! So I now turn to the question of how we should decide to allocate our limited attention.

4 Media Panics within the Supply and Demand Framework

The Supply and Demand Framework is useful in situating these YouTube phenomena, both as part of the overall YouTube System (itself embedded within the larger sociotechnical contexts of the production and consumption of media) and with respect to existing academic theories and empirical evidence bases.

My position, as I suspect the reader can infer, is that the Rabbit Hole approach is less fruitful in both respects. The phrase implies that the algorithm tends to recommend extreme or nonmainstream media, leading users down a "rabbit hole" into which they become trapped, watching countless hours of alternative media content and becoming hardened opponents of liberal democratic values and mainstream institutions. Granting the premise that YouTube was (and, to a lesser extent, is) an important space for radical politics, I argue that a model of YouTube media effects that centers the recommendation engine is implausible, an unfortunate update of the "hypodermic needle" model (Lasswell, 1927).

The "rabbit hole" theory is at a minimum incomplete, and potentially misleading. It did not emerge from communications theory, and as I will argue in more detail later, it is straightforwardly implausible within existing theoretical frameworks. One irony of the academic agenda is that the rigorous empirical and theoretical standards for academic publications render us less likely to produce attention-grabbing new theories or descriptions of empirical phenomena – thereby ceding this ground to the media panics.

Why, though, was *this* media panic so uniquely effective at capturing the attention of the study of media and politics on YouTube?

I don't know! The study of academic agenda setting is far from mature. I can speculate that the social power of a NYT op-ed compared to a Medium post was pivotal, or that Tufecki's argument fit better with existing academic literature or the intuitions of influential readers. Or perhaps Bridle's framing was too radical: "Automated reward systems like YouTube algorithms necessitate exploitation in the same way that capitalism necessitates exploitation" is ideologically stark. Maybe the evocative graphic design of the eyeball being radicalized was the more effective clickbait.

My preferred explanation for the success of the "rabbit hole" idea is that it implies an obvious policy solution – one which is flattering to the journalists and academics studying the phenomenon. If only Google (which owns YouTube) would accept lower profits by changing the algorithm governing the recommendation engine, the alternative media and thus the political extremism it causes would diminish in power. This is wishful thinking that undersells the revolutionary importance of YouTube as a novel platform for political communication.

Using a variety of different approaches, none of the academic research on the role of the YouTube algorithm in the promotion of extremist videos finds anything remotely like the provocative "rabbit hole" hypothesis (Brown et al., 2022; Hosseinmardi et al., 2020; Ledwich and Zaitsev, 2020; Ledwich, Zaitsev, and Laukemper, 2022; Ribeiro et al., 2020).

In short, the best quantitative evidence available demonstrates that any "radicalization" that occurs on YouTube happens according to the standard model of persuasion: People adopt new beliefs about the world by combining their prior beliefs with new information (Coppock, 2021; Guess and Coppock, 2020). People select videos about topics that interest them; if political, they prefer information that is at least somewhat congenial to their prior beliefs (Stroud, 2017). Persuasion happens at the margins when it does happen.

It is heartening to see that science works, at least internally: These disparate authors and approaches have tested the hypothesis empirically and converged on an answer. But again, this quantitative effort has failed to convince people to stop saying "YouTube rabbit hole." Even according to the internal logic of social science, those efforts could and *should* have been devoted elsewhere.

In addition to a poor use of scarce academic resources, the reification of the "rabbit hole" hypothesis is normatively troubling. The relationship between facts and values, between positive and normative knowledge, is a hotly contested one. I will not take a stance on this debate except to note that I think that both normative and positive concerns are relevant to setting the academic and journalistic agenda.

Consider the *New York Times* investigative report titled "The Making of a YouTube Radical" (Roose, 2019), which was so popular that reporter Kevin Roose spun it off into an eight-episode podcast titled "Rabbit Hole." From the transcript of the final episode:

First, we know that the internet is largely being run by these sophisticated artificial intelligences that have tapped into our base impulses, our deepest desires, whether we would admit that or not. And they've used that information to show us a picture of reality that is hyperbolic and polarizing and entertaining and, essentially, distorted.

And now there are even more of these algorithms than ever before, and they are getting even smarter ... what we have is a situation where the A.I.s keep showing us this distorted reality. And then we keep paying attention to that. And in doing so, we are telling them that we would like to see more of this distorted reality.

Journalism, like more formal social sciences, involves a rigorous epistemology, one that in this case is able to undermine the titular algorithm-forward frame of the podcast. Indeed, the rest of the podcast serves as a counterpoint to the algorithmic perspective. Because the podcast is competently and fairly reported, it spreads its attention to all of the relevant aspects of YouTube.

The central narrative concerns Caleb, the young man who became far-right radicalized by YouTube and then came back from the brink. The origin story for Caleb is clear: He watched a video by right-wing propagandist SM that the algorithm recommended him, then watched a bunch more, then saw that creator go on Joe Rogan's podcast and got hooked on the larger alternative media ecosystem.

The relevant analytic question for the Rabbit Hole hypothesis is this: How different would the recommendation algorithm have to have been to prevent Caleb's radicalization?

A longer-term perspective on political communication reminds us that audiences were exposed to new content even in the absence of recommendation algorithms. This task used to be performed by humans, surfacing and recommending all kinds of media. Given that SM was a popular YouTuber at the time, is it realistic that any recommendation system – algorithmic or not – would have prevented Caleb from *ever* seeing *one* of these videos? That world sounds radically removed from the one in which we live.

Another implication of the Rabbit Hole hypothesis is that the algorithm matters because it keeps someone watching a certain type of content. This theory involves very little user agency, a completely passive person who continues to neglect to navigate away from videos they do not in fact want to watch. Compare, also, YouTube to earlier "recommendation algorithms."

For example, the "recommendation algorithm" employed by a given channel on broadcast television is: Choose one program to show after another. How different would Caleb's experience have been if YouTube's algorithm was the same as Fox News'? Or alternatively, if after watching SM once, Caleb had navigated to SM's account and just watched all of his videos? Not very different, is my prediction.

Furthermore, from an industry-oversight perspective, amplifying narratives about tech companies' omnipotent products is exactly wrong.

In an interview with YouTube CEO Susan Wojcicki, Roose is discussing the role of engineers and the algorithm ("then humans come in and sort of tinker with it to produce different results. Do you feel like when") when Wojcicki interrupts him to say:

"Well, hopefully we do more than tinker. We have a lot of advanced technology, and we work very scientifically to make sure we do it right."

She does not let even a slight minimization of their omnipotent technology slide; she goes out of her way to correct an offhand comment. Given that the CEO of YouTube is committed to centering the power of the "very scientific advanced technology" behind the recommendation algorithm, it is striking to note that the Rabbit Hole hypothesis has led many anti-tech activists to say the same thing.

The story of Facebook's ad targeting is similar. Facebook is deeply, deeply committed to the narrative that their data allow advertisers to generate larger effects by micro-targeting specific demographics or even people. Many criticisms of Facebook take this premise for granted, usually in the service of calling for government intervention as the only sufficient counterforce.

We don't yet have effective online platform regulation, but the knowledge actors nominally hoping to hold these powerful corporations in check have worked tirelessly to ensure that the public is aware of those corporations' technological omnipotence.

The critique made by Karpf (2019) of the public conversation about "digital propaganda wizards" sharply parallels my view of the public conversation about "algorithms":

> digital wizards [are] an emerging managerial class of data scientists who are capable of producing near-omniscient insights into public behavior. ... But [this story] has little basis in reality. Simply put, we live in a world without wizards. It is comforting to believe that we arrived at this unlikely presidency because Donald Trump hired the right shadowy cabal ...
>
> That would mean Democrats (or other Republicans) could counter his advances in digital propaganda with advances of their own, or that we could regulate our way out of this psychometric arms race. It is a story with clear villains, clear plans, and precise strategies that might very well be foiled next time around. It is a story that keeps being told, because it is so easy to tell.
>
> But we pay a price for the telling and retelling of this story. The problem is that the myth of the digital propaganda wizard is fundamentally at odds with the myth of the attentive public ... Cambridge Analytica was made famous

by well-meaning people trying to raise an alarm about the company's role in reactionary political networks. But I would urge my peers studying digital disinformation and propaganda to resist contributing to hype bubbles such as this one.

4.1 Phantom Audiences

As an alternative to the research occasioned by the Rabbit Hole hypothesis, consider the mechanisms illustrated by Bridle and "Elsagate."

There is very little comprehensive information about internet use among children, but it is increasingly common among younger generations to have had internet access for essentially their entire lives. This has been met with an explosion of new content targeted at people in the single-digit age range. The very young are incapable of being discerning (having just recently discovered object permanence, and still very much enamored of the idea of counting), but their presence in front of tablets touching YouTube thumbnails registers all the same with the apparatus as audience demand.

The quasi-algorithmic learning process being conducted by human content producers can actually happen with no human input at all. Most bizarre and disturbing are the channels that "do away with the human actors to create infinite reconfigurable versions of the same videos over and over again. What is occurring here is clearly automated. Stock animations, audio tracks, and lists of keywords being assembled in their thousands to produce an endless stream of videos."

Here is the clearest existence proof of demand creating its own supply. There is no intentionality in the production process, just pure pattern matching. If the fourteen-month-old set stopped using YouTube, these videos would stop being produced, quickly. Even though these videos have millions of views, the argument that the influence is unidirectional from video producers to video consumers – the same argument that is taken as a given when discussing "radicalization" – is manifestly implausible in this case. There is no reason that so many of these nonsense videos would have been created in the absence of public measures of audience demand in the form of pre-rationalized YouTube viewcount metrics.

4.2 Qualitative Knowledge Comes First

Qualitative research is necessarily the first link in the chain of knowledge production. As Bridle's Medium post demonstrates, this does not need to take the form of academic publication. Although the cliché that professors learn just as much from their students as vice versa does not describe my experience teaching undergraduates introductory Python, I have frequently benefited from classroom informants describing their experience with digital media.

Qualitative social science is, of course, immensely valuable for theory building, understanding mechanisms, and transcending the researchers' preexisting categorization of the social world. It is essential that we not take for granted the frames that powerful actors use to describe our objects of study.

But quantitative research is likewise necessary. The media technology of human experience condensed into linear text is insufficient to grapple with the scope of digital media. Bridle doesn't want his article to be simply an "endless list of examples, but it's important to grasp how vast this system is, and how indeterminate its actions, process, and audience." He frequently invokes aggregate view counts in the billions.

This is one of the central limitations of the media panic as a mechanism for setting the academic agenda. It can effectively turn "unknown unknowns" into "known unknowns," but it is largely unable to communicate quantitative information like *scale*, *magnitude*, and *duration*.

4.3 Quantitative Description Comes Second

This is why qualitative description must be complemented by rigorous quantitative description as the second stage of the academic research process. This is the primary method I deploy in this Element; indeed, advancing quantitative description is a significant part of my current research programme (Munger, Guess, and Hargittai, 2021). Where political science once spent the overwhelming majority of its attention to the task of "mere description," in Gerring (2012)'s ironic phrase, the past few decades have seen causal research take up close to 100 percent of our efforts.

There is a reasonable case to be made that this is the natural progression of a discipline whose ultimate goal is to explain political phenomena: We initially needed to describe what was going on, but now that we have established processes like expert surveys, public opinion polling quantitative text analysis, and ideological scaling with roll call votes, we can treat this part of the research process more or less as settled. Even granting the existence of this progression, I argue that we are still allocating insufficient efforts to qualitative and quantitative description. If our objects of study were like physics or chemistry in that they were essentially stable (on the relevant time scale), we wouldn't need novel description: We could simply iterate between theory and experiment.

But politics is *not* stable, not even close. So we need descriptive research to tell us first *what is*, and then *what is changing*. I believe that social media is so radically unstable that we should spend much and perhaps *most* of our time simply describing it. Theoretical synthesis and then the *application* of knowledge is the ultimate goal, but social science (like social media) is a dynamic process with no beginning or end. Theory is thus also the first step, used to direct our attention and carve up the social world.

I find these meta-scientific considerations endlessly fascinating. But this Element is titled *The YouTube Apparatus*, so in fairness to my readers I must now turn to the specific theoretical framework that informs the empirical exercises to come.

5 The Apparatus

Figure 1 presents my Supply and Demand Framework as applied to the case of the YouTube Apparatus. My use of this somewhat abstruse term is inspired by Czech-Brazilian media theorist Vilém Flusser. Although he died in 1991, I have found Flusser's work to be incredibly generative when applied to contemporary social media. In *Communicology,* first published in English in 2022, Flusser describes how contemporary communication, mediated by digital images, cannot be understood through traditional categories but instead through what he calls the "apparatus-operator complex" (Flusser, 2022).

Rather than communicating with other humans with the intention of conveying some meaning, the apparatus reduces humans to mere *operators*, taking inputs from and supplying outputs to a system they cannot comprehend. The communication that takes place when mediated by this apparatus–operator complex is problematic – not intrinsically, but certainly with respect to the ideals of liberal democracy because it does conform the linear, logical mode of the written text that underlies our ideological and political system.

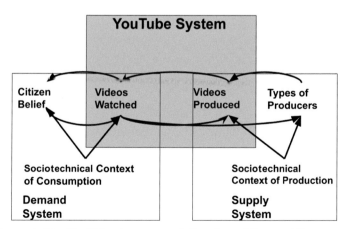

Figure 1 The YouTube Apparatus: A Supply and Demand Framework

This is all very woolly-headed, very Theoretical, but Flusser's metaphor is a useful bridge between the hegemonic Economics metaphor of Supply and Demand and the case of platform-mediated digital communication. Specifically, it makes the case that attempts to understand this kind of communication linearly are doomed to fail. The effects of communication on the operators are reciprocal; if anyone is being radicalized, it is because producers and consumers are *radicalizing each other*.

A crucial implication of this premise is that the medium of communication between these two types of actors is asymmetric. Consumers are watching visual media, something that most people have been used to doing since birth; some of the most popular YouTube content consists of vlogs, videos of a person speaking into the camera and delivering a verbal argument. For all but the most alienated, YouTube videos comprise only a fraction of their total media and interpersonal communication diet.

In contrast, producers are primarily consuming *audience metrics*. I discuss this at length in the following section, but it is important to note that this is a relatively unfamiliar form of media, something that only corporate media and advertising professionals were likely to encounter before the advent of social media.

In other words, the people who make up the Demand System are relatively less invested in the YouTube Apparatus than are the people who make up the Supply System. We should thus expect larger effects on the producers than on the consumers. We should expect that Demand creates its own Supply, and that these two systems interact through the YouTube System.

Figure 1 displays this interaction, the constitution of the YouTube Apparatus through the three interlocking Systems of Supply, Demand, and the YouTube platform itself.

This kind of cyclical diagram is unable to isolate specific causal effects – contrast with the explicitly "Directed **Acyclical** Diagrams" commonly used in causal inference (Pearl, 1995) – and is best thought of as a *process* unfolding rather than a description of a static reality.

These diagrams are less common today than during the heyday of cybernetics and systems theory in the social science of the 1970s and 1980s. As I will discuss, the most immediate and comprehensive predecessor to my current model is the audience theory developed in Webster (2014), and I am heartened to see that Webster's Figure 1 shares the same skeleton as the model I develop here. In the realm of public opinion and public policy, the thermostatic model of Wlezien (1995) and Soroka and Wlezien (2010) is premised on the same reciprocal kind of relationship.

One of the key challenges in deploying a model like this is the overwhelming complexity: For a given research question or area of interest, many more nodes and arrows could be added. I have attempted to retain only the pieces that I think absolutely essential. I am inspired in this regard by the central cyclical diagram in Soroka and Wlezien (2022) – an update of the considerably more baroque diagram from Karl Deutsch's model of the Nerves of Government (Deutsch, 1963) – which carefully considers each of the included arrows and nodes.

Accepting the premise of the diagram, a change in any of the nodes (descriptive questions about *what is*) or the arrows (causal questions about *what it does*) can ultimately redound to any quantity of interest. So if our goal is to understand how YouTube affects public opinion in the United States, we should aim to understand not just the well-studied *VideosProduced → VideosWatched → CitizenBelief* part of the causal chain, but the entire upstream system.

In keeping with my meta-goal of setting the academic agenda, I will primarily be discussing the components of the system other than this Videos to Citizen Belief pathway. In particular, my emphasis will be on the *VideosWatched → VideosProduced* and *VideosWatched → TypesofProducers* arrows on the bottom of Figure 1, the reciprocal side of the original relationship. This Element does not offer any original research on how the changing sociotechnical contexts of supply and demand have affected the respective components of the overall system, but I will summarize existing evidence in this area.

What I will *not* do is attempt to provide a quantitative answer to the question of the relative effect of supply and demand in this system. The central question posed by the paradigm of "agenda setting" is precisely this: Who decides what the system talks about or considers important? Does the media still tell the public what to think about, or does the public now tell the media what to talk about?

Any serious analysis of the system must conclude that it's *both*. Perhaps a more mature area of study could aim to answer this question empirically. Barberá et al. (2019), for example, analyze the relative agenda-setting power of US legislators and their constituents, finding that legislators tend to follow rather than to lead. And Wlezien (2023) finds that public opinion tends to predict news coverage more than the opposite relationship. We have much more robust methods, theories, and models for understanding the legacy news media (in the form of newspapers and television) and for understanding Twitter politics than we do for YouTube politics, so it seems reasonable to attempt to answer these questions about relative importance of supply and demand in those media domains.

I do not think, however, that these questions can ever be answered *conclusively*. We could find that for a given point in time and population of channels, 75 percent of the variance in what is talked about on

YouTube is driven by audience demand and 25 percent by producer preferences. Accepting the premise of the diagram, these numbers are intrinsically conditioned by both the larger sociotechnical context and by the specific affordances of the YouTube platform. Without a detailed and indeed quantified understanding of these other factors, we cannot plausibly hope to generalize these numbers to either other platforms or to an uncertain future. For this reason, I do not believe that careful causal estimation of a single or pair of effects is an efficient use of our scarce resources: The resulting knowledge is too expensive and too low in temporal validity (Munger, 2019).

By spending so much of the academic agenda on the *Elite → Mass* direction of media influence, we are not telling other academics, students, and policymakers what to think – *but we are telling them what to think about.* The quantitative exercises in Barberá et al. (2019) and Wlezien (2023) are thus immensely valuable not because of the specific point estimates they generate but for emphasizing the existence of the *Mass → Elite* direction of influence *at all.*

My hope is that the theoretical, historical, and qualitative evidence I provide in the following section will convince the reader that this is indeed an important relationship. Although I am intentionally agnostic about the relative effect of supply and demand within the YouTube System, it is safe to say that the effect of the Supply System on YouTube is greater than the effect of YouTube on the Demand System. The only path for the latter influence to take is when consumers view YouTube videos and change their beliefs and preferences – beliefs and preferences which are also affected by countless other phenomena in the social and political world.

The central substantive contribution is not a novel idea but rather the reinforcement of a very old one, summarized in what I hope will be a resonant metaphor: YouTubers are not "Creators" but *Creations.*

There is no perfectly clean delineation between the different portions of Figure 1; indeed, my goal is to render any clean delineation implausible. But for the purposes of expression in a linear format, it is still necessary to divide up my analysis into the three systems. I will discuss each of these in the following sections, but not in a perfectly symmetrical fashion. My discussion of each system will bleed into others because each section will bring a distinct literature to bear. We turn first to YouTube itself.

6 YouTube System

There are three distinct but related media system-level research streams that I will draw on to inform my understanding of the YouTube System. The first comes from Sociology and Communication, most centrally the work of James

Webster. The second comes from Economics, especially the work of James Hamilton and Matt Gentzkow. And the third is an interdisciplinary, network-driven approach developed by Matt Hindman. All three perspectives seek to understand the ways in which a media system mediates the relationship between supply and demand, each emphasizing illuminating different parts of this relationship.

6.1 Audience Theory

Webster's sociologically-informed approach begins by calling into question certain implicit premises of most research on media. The purpose of communication or media consumption is not necessarily persuasion or information transmission, but can be understood instead as a ritual performed to maintain some cultural practice. Classic research in this tradition analyzes the functional use of television as a social actor within the household; updated to the modern YouTube context, consider the meme that goes something like "Zoomers trying to eat a single meal without a mediocre YouTube video playing in the background challenge (IMPOSSIBLE!)"

Webster (2014) provides a comprehensive overview of the theory of *audiences*. The audience is a deceptively slippery category of actor, created not simply by the interaction between a consumer and a media object but rather by how the creator of that media object (or some other actor) understands the mass of consumers' interaction with that media object. The isolated media effects experiment conducted in a controlled lab does not fully capture "the audience" for that media object as either an ontological or conceptual category.

Webster (2011) adapts the sociological theory of structuration (Giddens, 1986) to understand the audience as downstream of the fundamental Duality of Media: "duality is a process through which agents and structures mutually reproduce the social world … the structures that agents use to accomplish their purpose are not static, but reflect the work of institutionally embedded actors who constantly monitor and adapt to user behavior" (p45).

Audience structuration requires seeing the act of media consumption through a different lens than that of the liberal ideal of the individual citizen becoming informed in order to fulfill their democratic duties. We're not talking about deliberating reasoners but about socially, technologically constructed aggregates.

The crucial questions posed by this approach are thus not the standard economics "what happens, and how do rational actors respond?" but rather "what kinds of information do actors have? What concepts are relevant to their perception and interpretation of this information?" Most important for my understanding of YouTube audiences are the concepts of *public* and *private* measures. These quantified measures are the mechanism by which audiences are *constructed* in the minds of those with access to those measures.

"Public measures that distill and report user information," Webster argues, are a "pivotal mechanism that coordiantes and directs the behaviors of both media providers and media users" (p43). Public measures circulate among all sorts of actors, and include things like university rankings and academic journal impact factors. These measures act as currencies that facilitate exchange and comparison, and while they are most effective when generated by some "objective" process or trusted third party, they cannot in fact be fully "objective" in the sense of apolitical. The very existence of these measures changes the behaviors of the agents and thus of the structures they mutually co-create.

Unidirectional causal inference, the primary goal of much contemporary social science, is simply implausible in Webster's framework. "Actions, freely taken, are the input for user information regimes that continuously structure and direct subsequent action. It is a process of reciprocal causation that evolves in real time" (p52).

There is thus a powerful irony in his categorization: The public measures designed to serve the interests of media producers in fact operate as a vehicle for agency among the consumers The user information regimes, in contrast, guide and inform the actions of the consumer while simultaneously creating digital trace records of great interest to advertisers and thus to producers. In summary, Webster argues that audience measurement is the "mechanism through which audiences cause the media to change" (p27).

The "Demand System" is an example of what Webster (2011) identifies as a "user information regime." For a given social media platform, this primarily consists of the publicly-available measures about different creators and pieces of content, in addition to the non-quantified information signals that creators send in order to attract audience attention. It follows that the "Supply System" is understood through a "market information regime" composed of viewcounts, likes, user comments on videos and other forms of qualitative commentary on given creators, videos or topics.

In the case of YouTube and many other social media platforms, these two regimes contain some of the same public measures. All involved actors are aware of the number of views, subscribers and likes that different videos and channels have, and they use this information to make decisions about what to consume or what to produce.

Personalized information – "private measures" – also plays an important role in each of the respective systems. Algorithmic recommendation of content, derived from users' previous consumption habits and from the multitude of data tracking systems embedded at various levels of the technological stack, provides the user information about what the platform "thinks" they might like to consume, as well as providing a shortcut to make these selections cognitively and temporally "cheaper."

The dominant concern about recommendation algorithms has historically been that they would reinforce the rich-get-richer dynamic. Through various iterations of the internet, from the earlier era of Google's PageRank algorithm based on incoming links and the blogosphere to the more recent social media built on an explicitly constructed social graph, the primary difference between the internet and either newspapers or broadcast media is that algorithms make audience inequality *more extreme* (Hindman, 2008, 2018). This is reflected back in the experience of users. "Virtually all user information regimes privilege popularity", (Webster, 2014) concludes – making it surprising that the primary theory of the YouTube algorithm is that it draws users *away* from the mainstream into niche Rabbit Holes of unpopular content.

Earlier shifts in the technological environment, and corresponding responses among both producers and consumers, prove illustrative. Consider what happened when Nielsen rolled out their new "local peoplemeters" (LPMs) as a technology for "objective" audience measurement. Audiences are intensely aware of the relationship between measurement and the actions of media producers; a public interest group called "Don't Count Us Out" argued that these new LPMs would undercount media consumption by minority viewers and therefore result in less television targeting those viewers. Ironically, this campaign was supported by funding from Rupert Murdoch's NewsCorp, which believed that they would lose out on advertiser's dollars under the new technological approach.

The evolution of these audience measures is thus best understood as a kind of contestation. No measure is perfect because there is no "real" audience; audiences are constructed through measurement. It is true that new technology tends to produce more detailed and extensive information, but different measures are still necessarily political in the sense of serving different purposes.

For example, the standard measure of television audiences is a binary measure of *viewership*: The LPMs record how many households have the television on and turned to a given channel when a given program is being broadcast. This makes sense as part of a media economic system financed by advertisers deciding how much to pay to broadcast an ad for the purposes of raising general awareness and approval of their product.

But for other goals, in other financing models, different measures could be more effective. Nelson and Webster (2016) describe these competing audience measures as forms of "currencies" that are more valuable when exchanged for different services. Using web tracking data from comScore, they find that audience size and engagement (time spent) measures are uncorrelated. The enhanced ease of direct-conversion advertising sales on digital media – advertising that entices consumers to click through and immediately make a purchase – makes engagement measures more valuable as currency for advertisers using this business model.

This economics-inflected analysis largely ignores the sociological processes by which media organizations acquire, analyze, and act upon knowledge of their audiences (Beniger, 2009). These processes are of course essential microfoundations for any incentive-based model of media organization behavior, and crucially for the application of my framework, these internal processes are themselves affected by changing technology.

This is not to say that different social structures cannot change how these analytics are used. Christin (2020) demonstrates stark differences in the reliance on audience analytics by United States and French media companies. The former (for historical reasons explored below) have relied on professional prestige networks to shield journalistic practice, while the latter have more fully incorporated these audience numbers into their workflow and evaluations.

Many of the following insights and references are taken from Napoli's (2011) excellent book on the topic of audience evolution. From the beginning of the medium, video-based media organizations have experienced conflict over the process of generating audience data and using it to guide their creative decision-making. In the early days of the film industry, executives relied on "fan mail" to supplement their then-spotty data on ticket sales in evaluating the reception of their movies, sometimes measuring the response in terms of pounds and ounces rather than reading them all.

One major concern of media organizations about the use of viewer letters as a source of information is that letter-writers are a decidedly nonrepresentative sample of the viewership. Napoli cites British audience research Robert Silvey's account of this process at the BBC: There were "seeds of doubt … when it became quite apparent that the overwhelming majority of letters came from middle-class writers … that while many letters began 'I have never written to the BBC before,' others came from people who wrote so often that they might be called BBC pen friends" (p34).

YouTube creators' internal analytics data come prepackaged; they're impossible for creators to miss and difficult for them to ignore. But this automated "audience rationalization" was not predetermined, and even the powerful data collection that underlies it is necessarily incomplete.

The immediate and highly specific and quantified feedback that creators of online content receive enables (and almost forces) them to figure out what the audience wants. The YouTube analytics that are baked into the platform – the public measures in the form of subscriber counts, likes and views – are both reified and challenged by the creators themselves. Christin and Lewis (2021) presents an in-depth analysis of a network of YouTuber creators who actively discuss these metrics, taking them as credible signals of popularity within their community while also arguing that they do not necessarily reflect underlying quality. The key insight, for my argument, is that everyone is aware of these metrics – and further, that this is public knowledge: *Everyone knows that everyone is aware of these metrics.*

In the era where simple exposure numbers were the primary currency for media organizations bargaining with advertisers over prices, there was little reason to care more about the opinions of rich people or devoted fans; neither of these tendencies was monetizable. For YouTubers, however, the diversity of possible monetization strategies and the importance of cultivating an active community gives them reason not to weight all audience feedback equally. A small number of highly engaged audience members can have a big impact on a channel's overall community, and a small number of wealthy audience members play an outsized role in determining a channel's revenue. It thus matters immensely who exactly these people are.

A recurring theme, both conceptually and empirically, is that the YouTube case supports different interpretations of existing theories based on how we decide to operationalize the categories on which those theories are based. The classic two-step flow model of media influence, for example, claims that the direct effect of "media" on "the public" is limited, but that there is a significant "indirect effect" that travels from the media to "local" "opinion leaders" who consume and interpret information to their "communities" (Katz and Lazarsfeld, 1964).

Conceptually, this model is either manifestly correct or completely undermined by the YouTube case depending on how we interpret these terms in scare quotes. Are politics influencers on YouTube who make reaction videos in which they give their take on emerging news "the media" or "opinion leaders"?

Even much more recent theories are not trivially relevant. Jenkins, Ford, and Green (2013) goes beyond Webster to emphasize the importance of participatory culture and "user-generated content," including the provocative claim that "the influencer is one of the major myths of the Web 2.0 world" (p80).

In the spirit of the Bennett and Iyengar (2008) critique, I find it instructive to ask whether these are useful categories at all. A social scientist primarily focused on determining whether an inherited theory is supported or not supported within an academic paper is justified in spending considerable effort working on these conceptual boundaries derived to explain a bygone sociotechnical context. But I am not this sort of social scientist. So we can simply move on.

The long-term trend in media duality, Webster concludes, is one of increasing *efficiency*. Better and more prominent public measures, created by structures that enable a higher density of decisions by agents and by technology that captures, synthesizes and applies those decisions, lead us towards the "triumph of convergence": a convergence of media supply with public demand. "Over time," he argues, "as digital media become more pervasive and the systems that power them more 'user friendly,' the distance between supply and demand will shrink" (p60). This predicted triumph of convergence can be rephrased as the triumph of the Apparatus, in which the internal information whirlpool of the YouTube System overcomes the possibility of exogenous shocks from the Supply and Demand Systems. Thankfully, in my view, we aren't there yet – but advances in media technology draw us ever closer to this bliss point.

6.2 Technology and Media Economics

I now explore how research on the economics of media in earlier technological, political and cultural contexts – what Williams and Carpini (2011) calls "media regimes" – can help situate the Supply and Demand Framework. The economics perspective is somewhat more narrow than the sociological one discussed above, with a strong presumption that media organizations' only goal is to maximize profits. The alternative hypothesis is that the owners of these media organizations have ideological goals as well, that they could be willing to trade off in exchange for lower profits. But the history shows the existence of a variety of different models of the incentives of the media over time. Very briefly, we can summarize these periods as party loyalists, profit-maximizers, and professionals.

The birth of the United States as an independent nation was intimately tied up with the circulation of news. Newspapers, which had previously been independent, were intensely politicized by the Stamp Act as a threat to their business model. The role of pamphlets, mail, and newspapers in the success of the Revolution led the Founding Fathers to give them special protections in the Constitution: The inclusion of the freedom of the press in the First Amendment was unlike any other nation at the time, and creation of the Post Office was one of the relatively few formally Enumerated Powers. This is the first of what Starr (2004) calls "constitutive moments" in the history of the media: A political choice over the formal and informal institutions that govern the use of communication technology.

Within this framework, Starr argues convincingly against technological determinism: that technologies are powerful but that the political response to them ultimately determines how they are used.

The second constitutive moment came with the emergence of the second party system, when Democrats responded to Andrew Jackson's defeat in 1824 by investing in a national network of newspapers. The resulting success, caused largely by increased voter turnout, drove other parties to adopt a similar strategy. Due to the vertical integration between parties and newspapers, the best model for the media in this era is that of party loyalists (Ladd, 2011).

Loyalist newspaper publishers had enormously strong incentives to promote party cohesion, to avoid idiosyncratic stands that could hurt the party, to build common infrastructure, and even at points to tack to the political center.

Skipping ahead a bit (Starr's book is the definitive resource for the interested reader), the development of high-volume printing presses and higher-quality, cheaper paper in the late 19th century created the conditions for a different media regime, one with striking parallels to the digital media environment of today.

These innovations in newsprint technology made newspapers into a major economic force. The two key engines of revenue were subscriptions and advertising dollars, both of which incentivized the curation of as broad an audience as possible. Subscription numbers were key for charging higher advertising rates, which in turn enabled a higher-quality product that would appeal to more readers. In this fiercely competitive marketplace, it was difficult for the previous round of party loyalists to maintain a large enough audience to offset new capital costs, and my quick history thus defines this media regime as dominated by profit-maximizers.[1]

These centralizing, audience-maximization tendencies became further pronounced by the broadcast technologies of radio. One crucial economic difference from print media is that broadcast media has essentially zero marginal cost for distribution; once the radio station is sending out its signal, it does not cost anything more for an additional consumer to tune in. But the reality

---

[1] This is a necessarily brief discussion of a complex historical reality. Kaplan (2009) provides a rich account of the critical election of 1896 as the catalyst that destroyed the prior media regime. William Jennings Bryant's candidacy was so polarizing that the previously Democrat-loyal newspapers abandoned the party; devoid of their prior source of legitimacy through partisan identity, they adopted the new logic of the Progressive movement. They were now public servants tasked with promoting the public good: "Liberal society needs a new, technical, selfless elite to administer it. This press model depends crucially on professional notions of supplying impartial, ethical public service against the corruptions of the market and the state. The profession carves out an autonomous realm for the exercise of its disinterested expertise against those who would subject social life to more instrumental calculations" (p35).

of a limited bandwidth meant that only so many stations could broadcast in a given time and place. This constitutive moment saw the federal government taking a much more active role in regulating broadcast technology than it ever had newspapers, in no small part due to implications for warfare. The Communications Act of 1934, in keeping with the general expansion of the role of the federal government in the FDR administration, established the Federal Communications Commission as the omnibus regulatory agency.

This institutionalization of the government's capacity to regulate radio shaped the response to advent of television, the most important media technology of the 20th century. The boom years after WWII saw increased demand for television, and the FCC took a strong stance on how the rollout should take place. The combination of technological limitations, intense federal oversight, and high capital costs meant that there were only three television stations in this period.

Because of these regulatory and technological restrictions, the media regime of the broadcast era was characterized neither by party loyalists nor profit-maximizers; instead, journalists and media elites were able to capture significant economic surplus. This took the form of some large fortunes by owners, but it mostly served to promote the professionalization of journalism (Carlson, 2017). Whereas they had previously been degraded as hacks, ambulance-chasers or sensationalists, the establishment of journalism schools, codes of ethics, and journalistic practice – combined with stable middle-class jobs and high-profile successes like the Watergate investigation – helped to raise the status of journalists to that of other professionals like lawyers or academics.

As Hamilton (2004) argues, news is an information good, and the normative case for traditional models of economic efficiency are designed around so called "normal" goods. This means that some amount of inefficiency (in the economic sense, inefficiences mean that supply and demand do not meet and thus that a given market does not clear) may actually produce better outcomes at the societal level.

The surplus value captured by journalists and editors was invested in the reputation of these institutions, allowing them to overcome the information asymmetries in the market for information. And the importance of professional prestige led journalists and editors to invest heavily in investigative journalism, in producing public goods like better information for all of society (Hamilton, 2016).

This "golden age" of American media started to end with the advent of new technologies that increased the number of available television channels, along with a loosening of regulations under the Reagan and Clinton administrations. The most important development was the creation of Fox News as an explicitly right-leaning cable channel. In parallel, the internet was developing into a powerful communication technology which initially repeated news from other media but which would go on to eat everything else. These regulatory and technological changes began to cut into the profit margin of existing media companies, eroding the nonpartisan, professional media regime.

The media environment today remains unsettled, and we will need quite a bit more historical perspective to neatly summarize it the way I have the previous periods But the most important development for the argument in this Element is the *individualization* of media prediction. The independent YouTubers with which I contrast the institutionally-affiliated channels only became possible with the advent of the personal internet and associated technologies.

The publication of formal analysis of media economics from the discipline of Economics has also shifted the academic agenda for studying media. This line of research applied to legacy media firms tends to *assume* that these firms are profit-maximizing. This follows from the tradition of general equilibrium analysis in Economics; in basic models of market-clearing efficiency, firms are forced to appeal to the median consumer or be out-competed, and there are enough firms in the marketplace so that none can make a profit.

Perhaps the most famous of these works is Gentzkow and Shapiro (2010), which measures the ideological slant of hundreds of daily newspapers from 1972 to 1998. They estimate that the variation in this slant is best explained by the ideological preferences of consumers; neither the explicit ideology of the papers' owners nor the estimated ideology of the editors has nearly as much explanatory power. Still, they are only able to explain 20 percent of the variation in slant, suggesting that there were (at that point at least) still significant barriers to a fully "efficient" market.

Gentzkow and Shapiro (2008) argue that a diverse media environment leads to greater investment in high-quality investigative reporting because of market discipline. However, in a chilling premonition of the present media environment, they also claim that "this mechanism will only operate if firms value a reputation for reporting the truth." The media regime of the broadcast era enforced that value on reporting the truth through professional norms and regulations, which combined to generate investigative reporting that served to advance "the public interest" in an epistemic check on the power of government and corporate actors. In contrast, the nascent post-broadcast media regime is losing this quality, resulting in "ruinous competition" between media organizations desperate to keep audience attention in a more crowded marketplace (Napoli, 2019).

Still, profit maximization cannot account for all media slant. Recent evidence suggests that in both the case of national newspapers (Archer and Clinton,

2018) and local television stations (Martin and McCrain, 2019), being acquired by wealthy conservatives increases national politics coverage and pushes the ideological slant of that coverage past the theoretical ideal point for profit maximization. This suggests that at least some of these publishers are acting as party loyalists.

Consider the case of the family of conservative billionaire Robert Mercer, who invested $10 million in the far-right website Breitbart.com (Mider, 2016). Breitbart is not a publicly held company, so its finances are private, but given the Mercers' political donations to other far-right causes, it is plausible that they would be willing to subsidize some losses to increase the supply of far-right online news.

Here is where "individualization" of media production poses a problem. Economic models generally assume large firms governed by internal bureaucracies and actors with disparate interests. This restricts these firms' capacity to even agree on a coherent ideology to express. In privately-held companies, owners do have the final say, but they are disciplined by their firm's reputation among other journalists, by their audience's preferences, and by the tastes of their staff.

The contemporary media era, which I have called "Clickbait Media," is distinctive in both the number of firms that are simultaneously competing for the same audience and the lack of institutional constraints on those firms. Munger (2020) models a world of web-native news firms producing online articles that are intended to be distributed on Facebook or other social media, but independent channels on YouTube can also be described as "Clickbait Media." Indeed, the term has been widely discussed by many YouTubers. David Dobrik, a popular YouTube entertainer, sells a line of clothing emblazoned simply "CLICKBAIT."

YouTube is stylistically distinct. although legacy news organizations retain their branding on their YouTube pages, independent news channels do not imitate legacy media aesthics. Instead, they seek to emphasis their originality, uniqueness and social identities shared with their audience. This is in explicit opposition to the staid aloofness of established news organizations.

This aesthetic is only possible because each "firm" can consist of a single individual, one whose face and personality is inextricable from their media output. The assumption of YouTubers as "firms" poses analytic and theoretical issues that limit the applicability of the standard Economics approach.

I find it necessary to draw this distinction because my "Supply and Demand Framework" is inspired by the Economics models. As discussed in Section 5, though, the assumptions baked into my Framework are specific to YouTube and other social media. Perhaps the most immediately relevant distinction is that Economics uses *prices* denominated in the uniquely powerful *money* to transmit information. The public audience measures on YouTube are effective at transmitting information within the YouTube Apparatus, but they lack the fungibility and the interoperability with the rest of society that money possesses. there are other differences implicit in the construction of my Framework, but the differences between prices and audience measurement are most theoretically salient.

Still, there are enough similarities that each of these two perspectives – the sociological and the economic – have provided different ways of conceptualizing the central portion YouTube System in the light of previous media regimes. Although I believe that the reciprocal nature of supply and demand makes the following division into a Supply System and Demand System akin to the chicken-and-egg question, there is analytical value in considering them separately.

While we don't know which came first in the grand scheme of things, we can be confident that *in America*, the chicken came first – domesticated in southeast Asia and then brought to the Pacific coast of the New World by Polynesians. Similarly, we can be sure that the first video was uploaded to YouTube before anyone watched any YouTube videos.

7 Supply System

We begin with the specifics of YouTube, which has more users than any other social networking site in the United States, according to Pew. while its lead over Facebook is growing, TikTok's explosive growth could represent the real challenger (Perrin and Anderson, 2019). This may be surprising, both that YouTube is more popular than Facebook and that it is even considered a social network. While some people use YouTube primarily to watch music videos or late-night comedy clips, the marketplace for original content on YouTube that serves as our focus is large, growing, young, and communal. In a 2018 interview, Google CEO Eric Schmidt said that "today we have quite a powerful social network embedded inside of YouTube" (Cowen, 2018).

However, YouTube is still frequently used by legacy media organizations to re-broadcast videos originally created for television, and this content tends to attract significant viewership. YouTube channels showing clips of late-night political comedy or prime-time cable news now represent important revenue sources for entities like Fox News.

This distinction is highlighted by another report on YouTube by the Pew Research Center, appropriately titled "Many Americans Get News on You-Tube, Where News Organizations and Independent Producers Thrive Side by Side" (Stocking et al., 2020). In the sample of 377 "news" channels with at least

100,000 subscribers as of December 2019, the two types of media organizations were roughly equal in number.

The report combines social media trace data with a *massive* survey of 12,638 US adults; surveys of this size and quality are out of the reach of most academics, but the scale is necessary to characterize media consumption in the era of audience fragmentation. This approach yields a similar result: Twenty-three percent of YouTube news consumers report getting news from each type of channel "often," and an additional 52 percent and 41 percent report getting news from "news and media outlets" and "independent channels" (respectively) "sometimes."

The impetus for the Pew survey was the media panic over YouTube as a locus of escalation in the prominence of far-right media in the mid-2010s. The presence of decently-produced videos from a constellation of tech-savvy agitators for the creation of a white ethnostate – and evidence of an active, engaged audience for those videos – was deservedly met with attention and anxiety. Where did these people come from, and what effect were they having?

Lewis's (2018) influential research on YouTube's role in American politics describes a group of political "influencers" who have attracted a wide audience by advancing a number of ideological positions in opposition to the centrist mainstream media. This research, in addition to journalistic accounts (Roose, 2019; Tufekci, 2018), prompted considerable academic attention to the question of whether far-right influencers on YouTube are radicalizing their audience (Ledwich and Zaitsev, 2020; Ribeiro et al., 2020).

The shock of the COVID-19 pandemic and demand for information (legitimate or otherwise) about it represented a similar re-organization of the YouTube media ecosystem, both internally and with respect to the larger media environment. The importance of high-quality information for the promotion of public health forced major reforms. So, at risk of oversimplification, it is helpful to divide the history of YouTube into four epochs.

From 2006 to 2011, a significant portion of original content on YouTube was produced by amateurs. Other than re-uploads of standard broadcast news and the noteworthy exception of the prolific The Young Turks network of progressive, organizationally-affiliated producers, there was very little political content. As late as 2009, there were fewer than 10,000 YouTube-original political videos uploaded.

Starting around 2012 and lasting until 2015, the second epoch is characterized by the entry into the marketplace by a small number of very active, amateur political YouTubers. This marked the beginning of native influencer media on the platform. Video production in this period was evenly split among left- and right-leaning independent creators, although the progressive Young Turk network continued to produce nearly a third of relevant videos during this time. In 2014, there were still only 44,000 relevant videos uploaded.

Brexit, Trumpism and the associated enthusiasm for culture-focused right-wing politics ratcheted up the partisan discourse in late 2015 and 2016, creating a feedback loop where demand for heated political arguments and takedowns increased This incentivized more entrepreneurial influencers to enter the marketplace, further increasing the quality of the partisan spectacle. There was a dramatic increase in the production of independent right-wing videos; around the 2016 US Presidential Election, they became the modal type of political video uploaded. By 2016, there were 87,000 relevant videos uploaded; in percentage terms, this doubling in production from 2014 to 2016 is the highest rate of change in the dataset.

In early 2019, however, YouTube took aggressive steps to reduce the likelihood that extremist or misleading content would be recommended by its algorithm (Buntain et al., 2021). This began the move to the current epoch, one of stronger enforcement of YouTube's guidelines and a suite of options (de-recommendation, de-monetization, suspension and deletion) for punishing channels that violated those guidelines. The end of the 2020 campaign and rampant and dangerous medical misinformation served as a test case for these new rules; although YouTube is far from perfect at detection or decision-making, the evidence suggests that the "Wild West" epoch is largely over. On the other hand, the COVID-19 pandemic caused a massive global shock to the production and consumption of digital media; a jump of nearly 50,000 additional videos produced, to a total over 200,000, from 2019 to 2020 was the highest growth in absolute terms.

7.1 Describing the Supply

To enable the longitudinal analysis of over fifteen years of data from one of the most dynamic media environments ever to exist, aggressively simplified classification is necessary.

I thus present a 2 × 3 classification of YouTube channels uploading videos to the platform.[2] My co-author on previous work on YouTube,

---

[2] We also coded an additional dimension. Borrowing Stocking et al.'s (2020) definition of a "personality-driven channel," we classified channels as personality-driven if they feature "a recurring host and orient their channel's content around the host's personality." (Stocking et al., 2020). If channels lacked a recurring host, they were not classified as personality-driven. Similarly, if a channel mainly consisted of audiovisual content with a consistent (albeit unidentifiable) narrator without references to any characteristic of the narrator, that channel was

Joseph Phillips, classified these channels by hand during the data collection process.

This classification is done at the *channel* level, meaning that all of the videos produced by a given channel are assigned the same labels. I discuss the limitations of this approach in detail below.

7.2 Organizational Ties

Building on Stocking et al.'s (2020) classification of "channel affiliation," we classified the organizational ties of channels dichotomously. Channels were classified as affiliated with an organization if the host had either explicit or well-known ties to legacy media outlets, advocacy groups, university lecture series, and/or party organizations, or if the channel itself represented such an organization. For example, Democracy Now! was coded as having organizational ties because the show began its run on the progressive radio station WBAI and airs on PBS and Free Speech TV. The Duke University Sanford School of Public Policy channel was also organizational as it depicts a speaker series for a university. Channels that lack such overt ties were not classified as organizational. Destiny, a prominent vlogger, is one such example. While he engaged in high-profile canvassing efforts in the 2021 Georgia Senate elections and the 2021 Omaha mayoral election, he did so without ties to particular advocacy groups or party organizations.

This division between organizationally-affiliated and nonaffiliated channels is crucial for our empirical approach. Although they each appear the same from the perspective of the platform architecture, these channels have different goals, capacities and audience expectations. YouTube is both a repository for previously-recorded videos and a social network connecting audiences with *YouTubers*, the independent political influencers producing original content.

7.2.1 YouTube, Pre-Social Network: News Organizations

These channels affiliated with news organizations constitute "pre-social YouTube": Videos intended to be distributed on a platform other than YouTube (most commonly, live television) that were then uploaded for asynchronous viewing. The Pew report found that 45 percent of these news organization

---

not classified as personality-driven. In total, 93 percent of channels were personality-driven in some form, and 7 percent were not; this category was, furthermore, strongly correlated with the dimension of organizational Affiliation: There were fewer than 1 percent of nonpersonality Unaffiliated channels, and this nearly empty cell rendered the 2 × 2 comparison trivial.

channels belonged to TV stations, 29 percent to digital-native news sites, and 16 percent to print publications.

Despite the hype around social media, it bears repeating that cable news is still *the* dominant force in American media. These channels are able to create videos with high production values beyond the reach of all but the largest You-Tube creators, and their decades-long reputation entrenches them against any upstarts in the minds of a slightly older audience.

Although YouTube has clearly empowered thousands of creators to broadcast video, it may also have the paradoxical effect of enhancing the power of established media institutions. YouTube allows them to expand their production because of the longer half-life for videos: There need never be a rerun on live television if the archives are all on YouTube. This in turn gives them more incentive to invest in *less* timely videos, in the hope of attracting viewership over a longer timespan.

Financially, legacy media firms receive a direct boon in form of a new capacity to "double-book" ads for a single piece of content, on broadcast and YouTube. Online ads are especially valuable because they dramatically decrease the barriers to "conversion marketing," where the purpose of the ad is to lead directly to a sale. This is key for maximizing profit from certain demographics; consider the types of products viewers of cable news are encouraged to "buy directly" by calling a phone number.

They are also less likely to respond to comments left on their videos, and many of them may even prefer to disable the social elements of YouTube entirely by banning comments and likes/dislikes. In this respect, the broadcast media continues to treat its audience like passive consumers of their content, even when the default setting of the new technology is to afford them interactivity.

These organizations continue to use the same logic they used pre-YouTube to decide what videos to create, and to rely on older models of media credibility based on source reputation and journalistic practice, rather than the accountability-based credibility of independent producers.

7.2.2 Youtube, the Social Network: Independent Producers

The more distinctively *YouTube* news channels are the independent producers. Ranging all the way from bedroom vlogs filmed on a laptop to interview/podcast-style shows recorded with high-end audiovisual tech, these channels developed out of the personality-driven YouTube-native aesthetic into the realm of politics.

The 2020 presidential election was the first major crossover between You-Tube Politics and mainstream electoral politics in the United States. Some of the most successful members of YouTube Politics are now household names. The insurgent candidacy of entrepreneur and political novice Andrew Yang was only possible because of famous YouTube figures. Yang said that "what launched us was Sam Harris. … Joe Rogan was the game changer … We raised tens of thousands of dollars a day for awhile there and a million bucks in a week" (Weiss, 2020).

Rogan drew a huge amount of media attention in late January 2020 when he endorsed Senator Bernie Sanders' candidacy. Rogan and Harris are both examples of what Lewis (2020) calls "micro-celebrities," attacking mainstream news and attempting to replace institutional brands with their personal ones.

These "micro-celebrities" or "influencers" have already been identified in the literature as more susceptible to the reciprocal *Mass $\rightarrow$ Elite* influence channel I emphasize in this Element. Lewis (2018) discusses the capacity of audiences to radicalize influencers by "enforc[ing] a type of accountability on influencers … [that] can *push influencers toward more extremist viewpoints*" (p39; emphasis mine). This argument is echoed by Philips and Milner (2020), who argue that "Conspiracy entrepreneurs *are also radicalized by their audience* … Content that meets the audience's growing need for conspiratorial content is rewarded by clicks and likes and comments and shares and subscriptions, generating revenue for the content creator." (ch4, p24; emphasis mine).

In both of these studies, this is presented as a bold claim, inverting decades of research on the agenda-setting power of the broadcast and newspaper media. Again, we see the dominance of the *Elite $\rightarrow$ Mass* channel of influence in the academic agenda. Ex nihilo, decades-old research premised on a bygone technosocial contexts is unlikely to describe YouTube today, but while there have been significant theoretical and empirical advances in the study of "hybrid" media systems (Chadwick, 2017), the literature has still been unable to fully transcend the shadow of longstanding theories.

Indeed, the term "influencer" begs the question. Recalling Webster's prediction of media convergence in the presence of increasingly immediate audience measurement, it would equally accurate to call them "vessels of audience desire." Once again, resonant metaphors dominate the conceptual agenda. Although YouTube encourages these independent YouTubers to call themselves "Creators," we should instead think of them as *Creations*.

7.3 Ideology

YouTube is ideologically diverse, and different sections of it attract (and are attracted to) different audiences (Munger and Phillips, 2022). Indeed, one of the primary novelties of user-generated video media is the unprecedented diversity of political positions represented. Unlike broadcast media organizations, independent YouTubers are unrestrained by internal ideological disagreement, expensive investments in reputation or hardware, advertiser-driven strictures of mainstream palatability, basic standards of journalistic integrity or even common sense.

For analytical parsimony, we developed a trichotomous classification. Channels were classified as "left-wing" if they advocate for a communist, socialist and/or anarchist system, redistributive economic policy, and/or socially progressive viewpoints such as support for LGBT rights and Black Lives Matter. Vlogger Destiny is one such example. Channels were classified as "center" as a catchall for minority ideological camps (like libertarians) or if they lacked an overt or consistent ideological slant – or if they styled themselves as "skeptics" or centrists concerned with perceived excesses of both the left and right. Once again, consider the Duke University Sanford School of Public Policy. Channels were classified as "right" if they advocate for socially conservative viewpoints like banning same-sex marriage, oppose immigration, identify explicitly as conservative, or advocate for white nationalism.

This approach, of classifying our dataset at the channel level, has significant drawbacks. First, if a channel underwent an ideological transformation (e.g. TJ Kirk moving from center to left, or Dave Rubin moving from center to right), it was coded as its most recent ideology: We looked at their most recent output and applied the same ideological label to their entire corpus. Still, we think that the base rate of this kind of switching between our three, discrete, categories is quite low. The median length of time for a channel to be active in the dataset is five years; using the rate of switching from center to left or right to center for media organizations in other contexts, we do not think that this is a disastrous assumption.

But even if switching positions across the entire ideological spectrum is unlikely, there are other limitations inherent in our simplistic coding scheme. These are certainly not the only three dimensions one can use to differentiate thousands of channels. Nor are these the only labels one could use within-category. For example, one could disaggregate centrists into "no ideological slant," "anti-politics," and "libertarian" groups. Much of the political "action" in digital politics and particularly on YouTube is the constant renegotiation of ideological categories. The culture-war issues that have come to consume mainstream right-wing politics were already stirring on right-wing YouTube in 2014; the fundamental (philosophically) Liberal value of free speech, championed by left-wing activists as recently as the Bush administration, was in the early days of YouTube associated with "skeptic" channels and has since around 2016 been associated with right-wing channels.

I should note that other scholarly efforts to categorize YouTube Politics have recognized this fundamental difficulty, deploying varying responses. My earlier work with Phillips was specifically investigating the "YouTube Right," with a time period that extended up until November 2018. We categorized this set of channels into three groups, with the caveat that "We do not think that these clusters can be fruitfully mapped onto a single ideological dimension; the dimensionality of the space is too high. However, we can comfortably rank them according to "extremism" (magnitude of the distance from the median on all dimensions): Conservatives, Alt-Lite, and Alt-Right" (p199).

This question of dimensionality is an important one I discuss in more detail below. But contrast out earlier coding scheme with the one used by Ribeiro et al. (2020). With a dataset that went up to 2017, they divide the non-left-wing channels into three categories: alt-right, alt-lite, and "Intellectual Dark Web" – a salient if ill-defined ideological movement that included the explicitly conservative PragerU, the explicitly libertarian ReasonTV, and the . . . . difficult to categorize Joe Rogan, who frequently hosts all manner of right-wing guests but who also endorsed Bernie Sanders during the 2020 US Presidential Election.

The decision over how to categorize Rogan, the former host of *Fear Factor* and currently one of the more famous people in the United States, is significant for the entire enterprise. His channel is the second-most-popular in our dataset. Following our coding scheme, the best coding for Rogan's channel is that it is ideologically in the Center (the catchall category for channels) and that he is organizationally Affiliated. The latter label is based on his historical connection to broadcast media. However, the case could be made that enough time has elapsed and that the fame of his original content has eclipsed his earlier career that he should be Unaffiliated. This problem is inherent in our coding scheme, but given the scope of the dataset, some concessions are necessary.

Returning to the literature, the most recent and in my opinion comprehensive quantitative analysis of YouTube Politcs as a whole comes from Hosseinmardi et al. (2020). Analyzing the period from 2016 to 2019, they divide the channels in their sample into six categories: five that range from Far Left, Left, Center, Right, and Far Right; and a sixth that they label the "Anti-Woke" cluster "defined in terms of its opposition to progressive intellectual and political agendas." This cluster has significant overlap with Ribeiro et al.'s (2020) "Intellectual Dark Web" cluster, and includes some of the channels that we had earlier classified into either alt-lite, conservative or even liberal/skeptic (and thus not part of the YouTube Right).

Hosseinmardi et al. (2020) highlight this terminological problem, noting that previous scholars had called some portions of this group "'reactionary,' 'anti-woke' (AW), 'anti-social justice warriors' (ASJW), 'intellectual dark web' (IDW), or simply 'antiestablishment.'" This final term, "antiestablishment," is what I have come to believe is the most useful.

Certainly, a refinement of the current coding scheme could deploy a video-based and continuous ideological scaling method like the one developed by Lai et al. (2022). While this approach has advantages over the current one, the use of sophisticated computational methods cannot remove the intrinsically subjective and protean nature of political ideology. The decision to reduce this high-dimensional space down to *one* dimension, in particular, is not an innocuous one. Although scholars of (particularly mass-level) politics in the United States have become accustomed to using the single left-right dimension as sufficient for scaling ideology, evidence suggests that a second dimension is becoming increasingly relevant.

Uscinski et al. (2021) provides compelling evidence for the emergence of this second, pro/anti establishment dimension in mass political attitudes. Crucially, scoring high in anti-establishment attitudes predicts increased support for both Bernie Sanders and Donald Trump – but predicts decreased support for Joe Biden. A unidimendionsional conception of ideology under standard Downsian assumptions cannot account for this non-monotonicity in preferences. This claim is consistent also with the decline of party identification and the rise of identifying as an Independent (Klar and Krupnikov, 2016), the renewed salience of anti-illectualism (Merkley, 2020), and the distressingly identifiable cluster of attitudes and beliefs characterized by Arceneaux et al. (2021) as the "Need for Chaos."

Taking a longer historical perspective, these tendencies can be seen in the lineage of the "paranoid style" in American culture and politics (Hofstadter, 2012), as the dark shadow of our bedrock faith in technology and Progress, our belief in our own self efficacy. The failures of the establishment – real and perceived – over the past decades, combined with the explosion in communicative possibility afforded by the internet, is a recipe for what Gurri (2018) diagnoses as nihilism.

Without falling too deep into digression, a meta-scientific note: *We are the establishment* in "anti-establishment," and the *intellectuals* in "anti-intellectual." There is no outside position from which social scientists can analyze the social world; this Element and all other academic research or public communication is inevitably fed back into the larger media and political environment. More than ever, "objectivity" is a false and dangerous pretense.

8 Demand System

There is a hard limit for the total audience for media: the number of humans awake at any given moment. Webster calls this "audience availability," the times and places in which it is possible for people to consume media. Arguments can be made for the possibility of consuming multiple media at once expanding this cap, and indeed I have first-hand experience of watching YouTube videos on one computer monitor while playing video games on another. Technological innovations have made it possible for more people to spend more of their time consuming media, and they have responded enthusiastically.

In addition to access barriers in the form of infrastructure and costs (both of which continue to fall quickly), a major constraint on the audience for YouTube videos is the distribution of preferences for their given medium or platform. There are some people who have a strong preference for written text; others prefer videos. The conditions in which people are able to consume media also matter: White collar workers have long been able to browse the web while at work computers, and many jobs involving physical labor now allow people to listen to podcasts or YouTube videos on their headphones.

The composition of the audience for YouTube Politics during the time period under study should determine the type of content that that audience demands. Walker and Matsa (2021) indicate that the overall audience for YouTube news (the composition of YouTube consumers who "regularly" get news from the platform) skews younger, more male, and less white than the country as a whole; in terms of political leaning, the audience is broadly similar to the national distribution, with a slight tilt towards the Democrats.

This is in stark contrast to some other social media platforms that have received outsized attention from academics and the legacy media. The regular news consumers on Twitter, for example, split 67-30 for the Democrats over Republicans, compared to 54-41 for YouTube. The difference in educational attainment is even more pronounced: 43 percent of Twitter news consumers have finished college, compared to 28 percent of YouTube news consumers.

The comparison with Facebook reveals different contrasts. Although similar in terms of age, ideology, and education, Facebook news consumers are 64 percent female (compared to 43 percent female on YouTube) and 60 percent white (forty-six percent white on YouTube).

Conversations about the different content moderation or algorithmic ranking procedures among these platforms sometimes miss these important baseline facts. From our perspective, with an interest in understanding the style of language produced and consumed by YouTube users, this demographic reality informs our expectations for YouTube.

The space of possibility for YouTube producers is far larger than that for consumers; the former could record a literally infinite variety of videos, while the latter are constrained to choosing among one of the hundreds of millions of videos already uploaded to the platform.

The decision about what to "click" on is the crucial micro-foundation of the demand system. There are many factors that contribute to this decision. Although scholars of political communication all know this to be the case, it bears repeating: The one overwhelmingly important criterion for the median media consumer is to *avoid politics*. Despite the fact that YouTube Politics is my main subsubsubfield of academic research, my YouTube consumption is dominated by music videos, recordings of live shows and Philadelphia 76ers highlights.

Once there is a nonzero chance that a user might choose to watch a political video, however, there are a number of factors that go into how they make that selection. The recommendation algorithm here is extremely important: this is a kind of "private measure" that the user can incorporate into their decision process. If we (accurately) model this process as less than fully rational and thus reliant on cognitive shortcuts, the simple fact that a video is *there*, on the YouTube homepage or the sidebar of another video, makes it much more likely that a user will choose to watch it.

Consider the other pieces of information available to the user at the point of "click." They can see the title of the video, the name of the channel, an image "thumbnail" from the video, and the number of views on the video – the latter a powerful "public measure" of the audience for that video. The importance of this decision and the paucity of information channels on which to compete has driven creators to compete to create "clickbait" titles and especially thumbnails; the reality of especially the latter has become something of a joke in the YouTube community, as everyone acknowledges how silly it is that creators are forced to select images of themselves looking shocked or elated in order to attract clicks.

But a significant fraction of YouTube video consumption is driven by the deliberate choice to watch a given channel or particularly *creator*. There are not good quantitative numbers on the exact proportion of these different kinds of consumption choices, but Hosseinmardi et al.'s (2020) web-tracking approach provides suggestive evidence that the videos reached via link from elsewhere on the web do not qualitatively differ from those encountered directly on the YouTube platform.

This is certainly consistent with anecdotal evidence of how people experience (at least the relevant portion) of YouTube. They aren't logging onto the website "to see what's on"; they want to keep up with their favorite YouTubers. An important update on Webster's audience theory in the context of social media involves the concept of community. People who are highly engaged fans of a given creator aren't just consumers, and they aren't members of an *audience*; they're members of a *community* or *fandom*.

Much of this difference is helpfully translated through the theoretical literature on media credibility as a major driver of media choice.

8.1 Credibility

The model of credibility empowered in the independent influencer sector of the YouTube media regime is described by Lewis (2018) in her seminal investigation of alternative media on YouTube. Lewis' model is based on the three dimensions of *relatability, authenticity*, and *accountability*. The former two are primarily stylistic, and match the narratives these alternative creators endorse about their position in opposition to mainstream legacy media.

Relatability means that they are more similar to their audiences, that they are able to explain the political world in shared terms. This dimension is similar to the rationalist explanation for why partisans trust sources that provide ideologically consonant information in Gentzkow and Shapiro (2006). In essence, each of us has a model of how the world works; if a media outlet provides media that fits that model, we infer that they are more trustworthy. The alternative, when presented with information that does not fit our model, is to infer that we are in fact mistaken about the world. "Relatability" works because lengthy, personalistic videos increase the dimensionality of the space along which the media producer can demonstrate that they share their audience's worldview.[3]

Authenticity is a direct inversion of the credibility of legacy media invested in a journalistic process that strives for objectivity or at least balance. Trust in media has long been on the decline and is now at historically low levels;

---

[3] There is also work in political sociology about the proliferation of nuanced cultural signifiers of a person's politics (DellaPosta, Shi, and Macy, 2015). The classic example is of "Latte Liberals," where the preference over a seemingly innocuous choice of consumption (style of coffee) is correlated with political ideology. Polarization has become more acute in the realm of "lifestyle politics," but not because conservatives' abhorrence of lattes has grown sharper. DellaPosta (2020) finds evidence of what he calls "oil spill" polarization: Lifestyle political alignment has become *broader*, encompassing a larger swath of lifestyle.

people no longer trust the process. Instead, YouTube creators emphasize their own subjectivity and their emotional investment in the topics they discuss. This authenticity opens the door to the para-social relationships that drive one of their main sources of revenue: in-video sponsored advertising, mostly for subscriptions to online services (VPN's, BetterHelp, etc.) or direct-to-consumer online goods (e.g. HelloFresh, Dollar Shave Club, etc.). Authentic YouTubers are able to charge advertisers a premium because they have cultivated an audience which trusts their views; corporations prefer this form of advertisement, which typically involves some modest discount code for signing up, because it allows them to track ad effectiveness.

Accountability, however, is the crux of my understanding of the Demand System. Lewis (2018) describes the process by which YouTubers are held accountable by their viewers, paying attention to their comments and continuing to provide a steady stream of content. This accountability can be extremely taxing for creators; legacy media accounts of non-political YouTubers experiencing "burnout" from the constant pressure abound. The stakes are heightened because another important revenue stream is another form of public measure. "SuperChat" or Patreon or related technologies allow especially invested viewers to pay extra in exchange for personalized attention or bonus videos. high-profile viewer dissatisfaction can threaten this valuable revenue stream.

There is a tension between authenticity and accountability that mirrors the central empirical question at issue: If creators are speaking their authentic truths, how can they also be accountable to audience feedback? I am personally bemused to see "authenticity" invoked as a criterion for what is ultimately and obviously a performance; to be "authentic" in the DIY/punk ethos of my youth meant to refuse to "sell out," to refuse to bow to audience demand and instead to remain committed to some higher artistic calling.

Of course, the fact that I don't "get it" may be part of the appeal. The "establishment" to which so much of YouTube Politics across the left-right spectrum is opposed is premised on this epistemology of objectivity. Joseph Phillips, in our discussions about the distinctive, appeal of YouTube, proposed an alternative way to think about the goals of the YouTube audience.

These are not people with a lot of agency in their day-to-day life, to say nothing of the political system in a country of nearly 400 million people. The centrality of *accountability* directly empowers viewers. comments on each video express approval or disapproval; if the creator makes some kind of misstep, either in their personal life or in the political positions they adopt, their audience can let them have it.

Scandals, cancellations and apology videos serve as the "media events" within communities of YouTubers and their audiences. They can set off chains of reactions, where other related YouTubers chime in on an issue; collaborative videos to address a concern; and audience reactions both on the platform and on other social media platforms. Despite (to me) the absurdity of the self-seriousness of everyone involved in what is literally a *performance*, this YouTuber/audience dynamic is at the core of the Supply and Demand System across the social world.

Journalist Jeremy Gordon analogized this media environment to that of professional wrestling. Yes, it's all fake: scripted and overacted, a strange farce of true physical competition. But a lack of faith in the larger system means that people believe that *everything is fake*. We might as well consume the more compelling fiction, the one that *takes us seriously*, rather than the establishment fiction which doesn't care about us at all.

So yes, I cannot watch political YouTubers as anything but the professional wrestling of deliberative reason. Normatively, I am confident that this is bad – that it degrades the quality of democratic politics. But it is unwise to treat this as a radical departure from previous political media. Postman (2005) identifies precisely these same dynamics as inextricable from broadcast television. And more recently, Askonas (2022) points to the famous confrontation between Jon Stewart and the hosts of CNN debate show *Crossfire* as a turning point in contemporary political media. Stewart excoriates the CNN hosts – one of whom was recent Vladimir Putin interviewer Tucker Carlson – for "hurting America" by turning politics into an ultimately bloodless sparring match. Or, as Vilém Flusser puts it, "we are being depoliticized precisely because politics pervade almost entirely the world we live in."

9 Describing YouTube Politics

At long last, then, it is time for the quantitative description of our dataset. Details of the data collection are available in the online Appendix – one crucial caveat. In the summer of 2019, YouTube changed the base limit for new API accounts to ten thousand per day – a 99 percent decrease. My API key's limit was grandfathered in, however, and I can still (as of March 2023) collect two orders of magnitude more data per day than new accounts can. There are no guarantees that this will continue, but I have taken full advantage. A project of this scale would not be tractable with the ten thousand unit rate limit.

Each of the 2,205 channels in the final dataset was categorized according to our 3 × 2 categorization scheme: Affiliated/Unaffiliated with a larger media organization; and ideologically left, right, or center. Table 1 displays the summary. A large majority of channels are Unaffiliated, with the right-wing Unaffiliated channels comprising the plurality of the dataset. Among each ideological cluster, the proportion of channels which are Affiliated is

Table 1 Categorization of YouTube Politics channels

	Affiliated	Unaffiliated
Left	127	590
Center	105	454
Right	171	758

remarkably consistent at 18 percent. The topline numbers show that there is significant ideological diversity in YouTube Politics, but that independent YouTubers outnumber affiliated channels around 4-to-1.

As I demonstrate in detail below, the audience share of YouTube (like all digitally networked media) is highly skewed, with the top channels commanding a disproportionate share. For this reason, and to give readers who are unfamiliar with YouTube Politics a taste of what these channels are like, Table 2 lists the top twenty-five channels by aggregate viewcount. The main trend that emerges from this list is the relative prominence of left-leaning and especially Affiliated channels at the top in terms of viewership compared to their share of the overall dataset. Only 36 percent of these channels are non-Affiliated, compared with 82 percent of the full sample.

Qualitatively, there are a few different clusters of channels. To really grasp YouTube Politics, I encourage interested readers to sample some of these videos; there is only so much that can be communicated about this massive and (again) video-based media environment in a few pages of text. Still, a slightly thicker description will hopefully add a bit of structure to the quantitative analysis to come.

One group consists of right-leaning channels which emerged from the larger conservative media ecosystem but which have embraced YouTube to connect with a younger audience than heavyweights like Fox News. The media company The Daily Wire is the center of this cluster, along with central personalities Ben Shapiro, PragerU, and the recently-independent Steven Crowder. With three channels in the top ten, this cluster is more of a formal network than a decentralized tendency (like the other clusters), and thus has managed to wield disproportionate agenda-setting power.

A prominent left-leaning cluster consists of early digital media entrepreneurs who have adapted to the YouTube environment. The primary audience for this cluster (in my impression, lacking concrete data) is the cohort of older Millennials and younger Gen Xers who became interested in the first wave of internet news during the George W. Bush presidency. The number one most-viewed channel in the dataset, The Young Turks network, exemplifies this

Table 2 Breakdown of top twenty-five YouTube channels

	Aggregate Viewcount	Ideology	Affiliated
The Young Turks	5,950,322,060	Left	Yes
PowerfulJRE	4,624,063,645	Center	Yes
VICE	3,219,362,881	Left	Yes
Breakfast Club Power 105.1 FM	2,814,646,184	Left	Yes
AsapSCIENCE	1,821,203,479	Left	No
PragerU	1,658,509,053	Right	Yes
h3h3Productions	1,542,454,821	Left	No
StevenCrowder	1,535,934,533	Right	Yes
Ben Shapiro	1,477,862,113	Right	Yes
Real Time with Bill Maher	1,437,791,479	Left	Yes
David Pakman Show	1,341,990,814	Left	No
Kurzgesagt – In a Nutshell	1,239,956,328	Center	No
Brian Tyler Cohen	1,204,322,303	Left	No
The Howard Stern Show	1,188,697,129	Center	Yes
Timcast	1,067,353,228	Right	No
NowThis News	1,062,052,728	Left	Yes
Cracked	1,024,294,846	Left	Yes
TheQuartering	1,024,181,609	Right	No
Secular Talk	1,012,533,913	Left	Yes
H3 Podcast	973,957,963	Left	No
The Ring of Fire	894,362,056	Left	Yes
DailyWire+	872,552,379	Right	Yes
Donald J Trump	833,107,641	Right	Yes
The Hill	823,065,971	Center	Yes
Iraqveteran8888	800,883,131	Right	No

cluster, along with former Young Turks member Kyle Kulinski (Secular Talk); The Ring of Fire, somewhat affiliated with David Pakman, is another major progressive-leaning YouTube network with roots in the Bush-era left.

Number three channel VICE has overlaps with this cluster as well, but their distinctive combination of progressive politics with somewhat risque reporting illustrates a difficulty of this classification exercise. The channel uploads original videos, many of which have either explicit or implicit political content, and thus fit the scope of our data collection strategy. However, not all of the videos are particularly political; the channel's most-viewed video is titled

"Making The World's First Male Sex Doll." Furthermore, the reporter-turned-pundit Tim Pool (Timcast) worked for VICE in the early 2010s, but is now distinctly right-leaning.

A third cluster consists of broadcast-era media celebrities who were able to translate their fame onto YouTube, generally with a talk-show format. Joe Rogan (PowerfulJRE), Breakfast Club Power 105.1 FM, Bill Maher, and Howard Stern all fit this bill, and their presence illustrates a continuity between YouTube and previous media regimes. Stern, for example, frequently featured live callers to his radio broadcast, a precursor of the YouTube comments posted by viewers. Of these four, Maher is the only one with a political focus; the rest frequently discuss politics, but tend to emphasize entertainment topics. There is a case to be made that the channel belonging to actor and media personality Donald J. Trump fits into this cluster.

A fourth cluster, considerably underrepresented here compared to the larger dataset, are independent YouTubers who simply started making videos about news and current events. These YouTubers tend to focus on topics of interest to younger men, including video games, guns and what is best summarized as "internet culture." The h3h3Productions and h3 Podcast channels lean to the left, while Iraqveteran888 and TheQuartering lean to the right. Like the previous affiliated cluster, these YouTubers explicitly emphasize something other than politics and are distinctly not "news organizations," but often bring a culturally political perspective to the topics they discuss.

Other clusters that are represented in this top twenty-five list include professional media organizations like NowThis News and The Hill, and science/education channels like AsapSCIENCE and Kurzgesagt. There are, of course, many channels in the dataset which do not fit neatly into any of these clusters.

Returning to the 2×3 categorization, Figure 2 displays some long-term evidence about the first step in the chain of evidence that leads to our downstream analysis of news quality: channel entry. This topline analysis shows that there was a significant bunch of channels begun in 2006 that remain active media organizations, then a down period for channel creation with only 75 new channels per year on average. From 2011 to 2014, approximately 170 channels joined each year, with significant year-to-year variation. The most prominent period for channel entry in YouTube Politics, however, is clearly the pivotal years of 2015, 2016 and 2017. The peak year was 2016, when Donald Trump's presidential campaign both spurred and revealed enthusiasm for online political discussion on YouTube.

Figure 3 breaks down the same data on channel entry by the organizational structure of the channels. Noting that the y-axes are significantly different

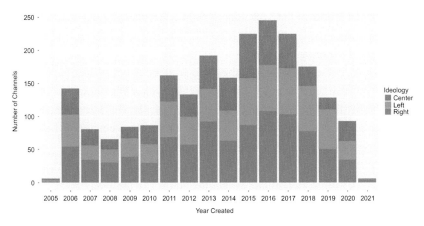

Figure 2 Channels entering YouTube Politics marketplace

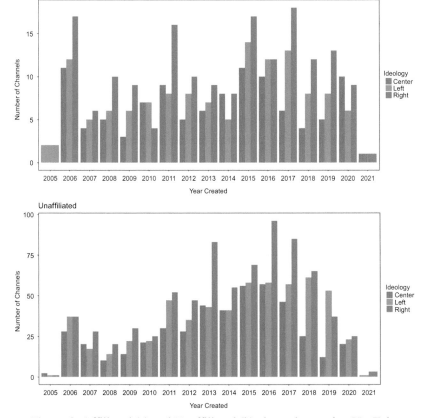

Figure 3 Affiliated (a) and Unaffiliated (b) channels entering YouTube Politics marketplace (note different y-axes)

in order to evaluate the relative rather than absolute trends, a few comparisons to highlight. First, the spike in 2006 channel creation is far more pronounced among the organizationally-Affiliated channels, reflecting the adoption of the new platform by tech-savvy media organizations like Vice News. Second, the overall growth in channel entry from 2011 to 2017 is primarily concentrated in the Unaffiliated channels, while both graphs show peak entry between 2015 and 2017. Third is the beginning of a significant advantage of right-wing Unaffiliated channel entry over left-wing Unaffiliated channel entry in 2013, peaking in 2016 but disappearing entirely by 2018, the peak year for left-wing Unaffiliated channel entry.

One key takeaway from the channel entry data is that independent political YouTubers seem to start channels counter-cyclically relative to macro-level political events. There is less data for affiliated channels, but the general pattern tends to be more pro-cyclical, reflecting rather than subverting the political media environment as a whole.

So the largest year-on-year increase in channel entry for left-leaning YouTubers was in 2011, the year after the Tea Party-led Republican wave in the 2010 Congressional elections. In contrast, there was no increase in entry by left-leaning Affiliated channels that year, but entry by right-leaning Affiliated channels *quadrupled*.

Right-leaning YouTuber entry increased the most in 2013, after Obama's re-election, and reached its peak in 2016 in parallel with the outsider Trump campaign. However, once Trump was in office, right-leaning YouTuber entry declined while left-leaning YouTuber entry stayed steady or increased. the only year that YouTuber entry was higher on the left than right was 2019.

Figure 4 uses the same channels to drill down on video production. Here there are noticeably asymmetric trends by ideology. Among Affiliated channels, there is a clear dominance in the production of left-leaning videos (especially in the first half of the time series, driven by the prolific The Young Turks network), and additionally a noticeable separation between right and centrist production. In contrast, among Unaffiliated channels, there was a large advantage for right-leaning videos, with a smaller number of videos produced by the left and center. The most distinctive trend in this cluster is a radical increase in the slope of right-wing YouTuber video production beginning in 2016 that plateaued from 2020 onward.

The topline results for the video consumption side are displayed in Figure 5. Here, the prominence of The Young Turks network is even more pronounced: Left-wing Affiliated channels were responsible for more than half of all viewership each month from 2009 until sometime in 2016. The striking growth in right-wing Unaffiliated video production in Figure 4 is still visible here in terms

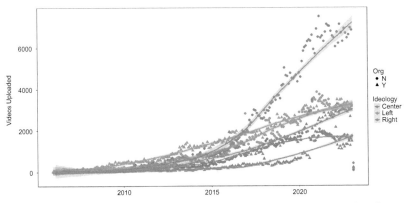

Figure 4 Videos uploaded by ideological cluster and organizational
affiliation, monthly

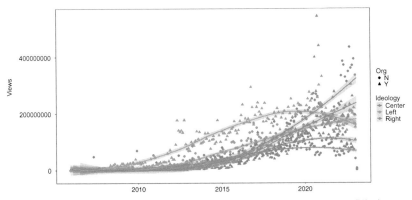

Figure 5 Total views by ideological cluster and organizational affiliation,
monthly

of views, but with two caveats: There is a considerable lag between the growth
in video production and video consumption; and the growth in video consumption is only slightly larger than the growth in video consumption for right-wing
Affiliated channels until 2020 .

These contrasts are thrown into sharper relief by Figure 6, which displays
the same viewership numbers in terms of the *median video* for each cluster in
each month. Again, the left-wing Affiliated cluster leads throughout the entire
time series, caught by the right-wing Affiliated cluster only at the very end. But
the striking difference is that the right-wing Unaffiliated cluster – the cluster
which produced the most videos every month from mid-2017 until the present –
had very low median views per video. The only cluster with a lower average
median views per video, for the entire time series up until 2016, is the left-wing
Unaffiliated cluster, which then grew steadily in median popularity up until the
end of the time series.

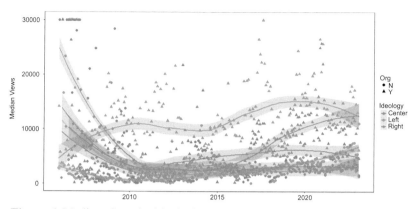

Figure 6 Median views by ideological cluster and organizational affiliation, per video

There are clear limitations to any given summary statistic of these aggregate consumption numbers. This dataset, after all, comprises 1.4 million videos from 2,205 channels over the course of fifteen years – 85 ***billion*** views in total. The total views in Figure 5 represent a combination of the number of channels in each cluster, the videos those channels produce, and their overall popularity. On the other hand, the median views in Figure 6 could be maximized by clusters in which less popular channels either decrease their video production or exit the marketplace entirely. So depending on the theoretical target of interest, any of these time series would or would not be useful tests.

However, much of the value of this quantitative description comes not from theory testing but from hypothesis generation. While the preceding analysis does not provide any definitive answers, it does call into question the received wisdom that YouTube Politics is overwhelmingly right-leaning, and I hope that the specific trends will inspire future researchers to ask more informed questions.

9.1 Other Metrics, Other Audiences: Engagement

Returning to Webster's theory of audiences and audience measurement, we can take advantage of the variety of metrics provided by YouTube's platform affordances. Thus far, we have focused on the viewcount metric. Webster notes that this is the most common strategy, as simple viewership is generally the easiest to measure and the most immediately relevant for media marketplaces driven by mass advertising. If your goal is simply to get your ad in front of as many eyeballs as possible, you're indifferent between programs that generate intense engagement with their audience and those that barely convince their audience not to change the channel.

For many purposes, however, it would be useful to measure other forms of audience *engagement* beyond the simple binary of media consumption. "The audience" is neither a static nor a homogeneous entity, and different media producers may inspire different types of engagement among their audiences. This is especially relevant when alternative monetization strategies are possible for media producers. Some YouTubers profit directly from the viewcounts thanks to YouTube's profit-sharing system, but this arrangement is particularly fraught for political influencers who remain at the mercy of changing content moderation standards. Most YouTubers, then, are invested in cultivating and maintaining an audience of highly engaged viewers who they could monetize directly, in the form of donations (tips), patronage (through private membership platforms like Patreon), in-video sponsored advertising, and direct sales of merchandise or other sponsored products.

The comments under each video are central to both measuring and cultivating this more intense engagement. Culturally, YouTube viewers tend to understand the comments section as a sort of public square where they are able to express their views; channels that ignore their comments section (or worse, turn off comments entirely – generally seen as cowardice) are prone to losing their most engaged viewers.

Figure 7 replicates the total viewcount per cluster per month from Figure 5, replacing views with comments. The broad trends are similar: Raw consumption (views) is a precondition for more intense forms of engagement like commenting, so it would be surprising to see completely inconsistent results in these two figures. Perhaps the most noteworthy difference is that Figure 7 demonstrates a much larger divergence in the rate of growth for the two right-wing clusters. While their growth in viewership was similar, the number of comments grew much more quickly for the non-Affiliated YouTubers than for the Affiliated channels. This is consistent with an important difference along this dimension in terms of both the strategy of producers and the experience of their audiences.

Again, no single statistic is perfect, so Figure 8 displays the evolution in the *ratio* of comments to views for each of these clusters. The median value of this statistic per cluster is shown in the top panel, and the mean value in the bottom panel. Here, the clearest distinction is between those channels that are non-Affiliated and those which are Affiliated, regardless of ideological leanings. The first half of the time series shows the left-wing Affiliated channels with by far the highest levels of engagement, although these statistics are based on only a small number of videos.

In the top panel, we see the left- and right-wing Affiliated channels catching up to the Unaffiliated channels in terms of median comments/views ration

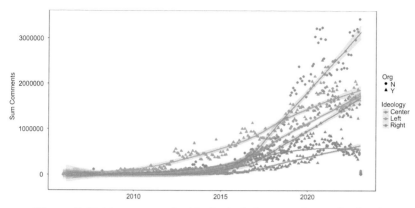

Figure 7 Total comments by ideological cluster and organizational affiliation, monthly

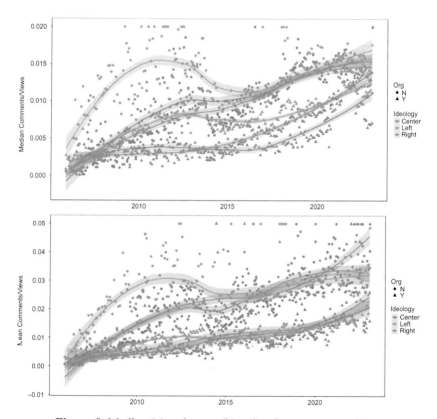

Figure 8 Median (a) and mean (b) ratio of comments to views

over the second half of the time series. The growth for the latter cluster is especially impressive: Their ratio nearly triples from .004 (i.e. 0.4 percent of views resulted in comments) to .012 between 2015 and the end of the time series.

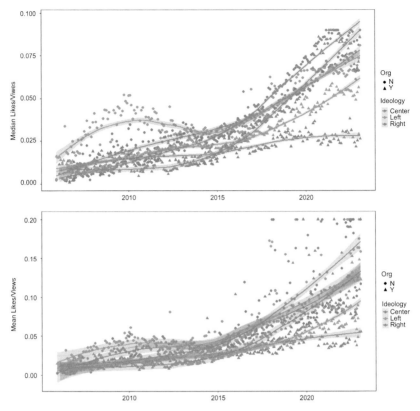

Figure 9 Median (a) and mean (b) ratio of likes to views

The mean values in the bottom panel show an even greater gap between the Unaffiliated and Affiliated clusters; here, though, the most significant growth comes from the already highly-engaged viewers of the right-wing Unaffiliated channels over the past two years.

Comments are the most intensive form of engagement that is hardcoded into the YouTube platform at the level of the individual video, but there is another metric between comments and views: likes. Made famous by Facebook's "thumbs-up" icon in 2009, the "like" is perhaps the minimal unit of approval across the social web. YouTube creators and audiences alike seem to recognize the like as a public signal of approval – visible to both other human users and to the recommendation algorithm on the platform side. Figure 9 thus replicates the analysis of the comment/view ratio for likes.

Once again, each of the Unaffiliated channels outperforms its Affiliated ideological partner throughout the time series. But compared to the comment ratio analysis, the increased intensity of engagement for right-wing channels over the past five years is even more pronounced. In the top panel, for example, the right-wing Affiliated channels go from the lowest median like ratio in 2015 to second only to the right-wing Unaffiliated channels by the end of the period of analysis. And here, in the bottom panel showing the mean like ratio, this right-wing Affiliated cluster catches up to the Unaffiliated clusters in other ideological groups. I've had to top-code some of these data points for visual clarity; the points at the top of the chart represent a like/view ratio of .2, meaning that fully 20 percent of the views were converted into likes.

The audience created by these more intensive measures of engagement is very different from the one conjured by simple viewership. Given the economic and social incentives facing independent YouTubers, I believe that these audiences shine more light on my central theoretical claim that Demand creates its own Supply. These YouTubers are not Creators but *Creations* of their audience, and the more intensive forms of engagement are that audience's most potent tool.

A further complication is the possibility that the individuals who make up the Demand System are *becoming more strategic*. Again, the dominant trend in the bottom panel of Figure 9 is that the like/view ratio for all independent YouTubers increases dramatically around 2016 after nearly a decade of being almost flat. This could reflect audiences' growing awareness of their control over creators, or it this could reflect something else entirely, about how the platform infrastructure for recording likes or views shifted. Again, these descriptive data, created at the intersection of the platform affordance and user actions, are not the final word. I intend them as rudimentary map of this vast and underexplored territory, one that will guide future explorers.

9.2 Economic Concentration and Dynamic Stability

I have argued for the utility of the Supply and Demand model for social media synthesizing micro-level changes at each point in a given social media platform and for developing hypotheses about how these changes redound throughout the system to a given outcome of interest. The model is also useful for making macro-level comparisons *across* platforms, with reference to well-established models of market competition in other media regimes.

The primary motivation for the following analyses comes from Hindman (2018), as discussed above. Crucial to Hindman's model of the marketplace for online attention are two macro-scale features of social networks: the *exponential distribution* (i.e. high market concentration) of attention across different media organizations and individual pieces of content, and the *stickiness* of the economic positions of actors over time.

The first point can be demonstrated by plotting the popularity of each channel against the rank ordering of that channel. For normal distributions, this analysis

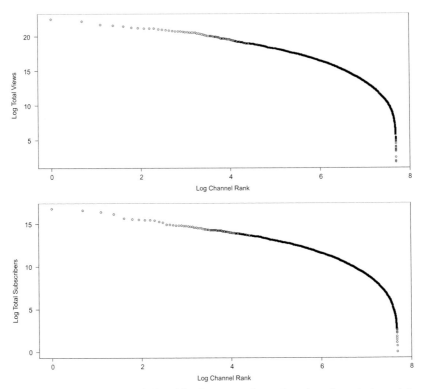

Figure 10 Log-linear relationships between channel rank and total views (a)
and subscriber count (b)

produces a roughly linear relationship; for exponentially-distributed data of the
sort driven by networked relationships, however, the relationship should be *log-*
linear. The topline results in Figure 10 demonstrate that the current data falls
firmly into the latter category. The top panel displays the relationship between
the rank and the total number of views the channel has accumulated; the bottom
panel is the same except for the number of subscribers.

The two graphs are essentially the same, with perhaps a slightly cleaner
log-linear fit for the total channel views near the high end of the distribution.
Both graphs show a marked sub-log-linear relationship for the least popular
channels.

I interpret this as a positive sign for the sampling and data collection strategy.
The fact that we encountered, coded and scraped data from channels this far
down the food chain suggests that the primary results of the analysis are robust.
In other words, it is extremely unlikely that there are channels that were missed
which were large enough compared to the overall YouTube Politics ecosystem
to meaningfully change the results.

As a robustness check, I re-ran all of the above analyses using only channels for which we had record of having produced more than the median number of videos – 175 videos per channel. This reduced the number of channels under analysis by 50 percent (obviously), to just over 1,100 channels. However, this reduced the number of *videos* in the dataset by only 6.5 percent, from 1.40 million to 1.31 million. This is the reality of exponentially distributed data; all of the inferences drawn from this smaller dataset remain essentially unchanged. The one graph with a notable difference is in the median ratio of comments to views (Figure 8, top panel), in which the left-wing Affiliated channels keep pace with the right-wing Affiliated channels in the latter half of the time series. This statistic is less weighted by overall popularity, and this cluster had the largest number of very small channels in the dataset. Overall, however, this re-analysis serves to both demonstrate Hindman's point about the inequality of these systems and to bolster our confidence in the findings thus far.[4]

Zipf's law visualizations like those in Figure 10 are useful for diagnosing a power law distribution, but they are not particularly high-resolution. To take advantage of the temporal component of the data, Figure 11 plots the Gini coefficient in viewership monthly. The top panel calculates this statistic (where perfect equality in viewership that month would be a 0, and absolute concentration would be a 1) across all videos, while the bottom panel aggregates viewership numbers for all the videos by a given channel each month before calculating the Gini coefficient.

The two panels show similar results in the first half of the time series: Viewership becomes more and more concentrated until a peak in the middle of 2012 and a gradual decline in inequality until 2015. This can be interpreted as evidence of the growing power of networked attention, driven primarily by the recommendation algorithm. Beginning in 2016, however, the trends diverge: The video-level inequality continues to decline over the next seven years, while the channel-level statistic levels off at an extremely high level of inequality. The former effect is almost mechanical in the number videos produced, the growth in which really took off in 2016. However, the trend in the bottom panel makes it clear that there is little democratization of attention away from the biggest channels.

---

[4] The converse of this is also true; however, my results are much more sensitive to the inclusion or exclusion of the most popular channels. In this case, the concern would not be that there were channels that our sampling frame did not detect, but rather that the channels we included should not fall into the scope of YouTube Politics. For example, the third-largest channel in terms of total views is VICE, which we categorized as left-wing and organizationally Affiliated. As discussed above, the ambiguity is a clear limitation of our approach to code our data at the *channel* level, and suggests that some of these ambiguous cases may be adding noise to our results.

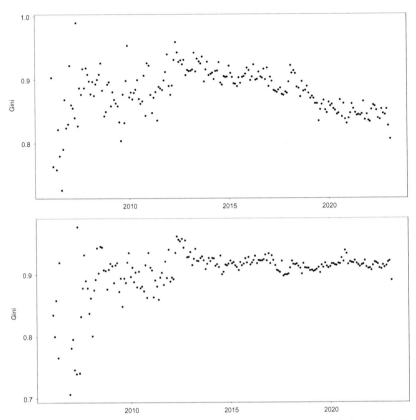

Figure 11 Inequality in monthly views across all videos (a) and channels (b)

This finding is suggestive of the second of Hindman's points, the stickiness or dynamic stability of the market positions of media producers. But we can get much more granular. Figure 5.4 in Hindman (2018) presents the key result: The market share of each website in his analysis is remarkably similar year-on-year. That is, the most popular websites tend to remain the most popular websites, in contrast to the folk theory of the instability of digital media.

I replicate this analysis for each of the year-on-year changes in my dataset for which there is sufficient data. Building on the aggregate results above, I include only the 75 percent most popular channels in each year in this analysis; the bottom of the distribution has so few views that the percentage change or rank change in their views can appear large even when the actual number of views is on the order of hundreds, rather than the thousands or millions of views for more popular channels.

Figure 12 displays these year-on-year changes for 2021 to 2022 – the most recent period for which I have full data. The four panels all tell more or less the same story: There is little mobility in popularity among the channels in the

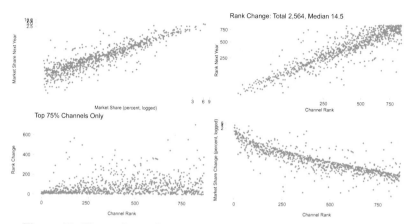

Figure 12 Change in market share (a), change in rank (b), absolute rank change (c), absolute market share change (d). Change from 2021 to 2022. 1,115 channels included in analysis.

dataset. The top left panel plots the absolute market share (as a percentage of total views) of each channel in 2021 against that channel's share in 2022; the bottom right panel is similar, plotting the *change* in percent of market share against the channel's rank. The top right panel plots the rank in channel viewership in 2021 against that of 2022, and the bottom left panel the absolute value of the change in rank against the channel rank.

The Young Turks channel, founded in 2005, is the most viewed channel in the full dataset, with 5.8 billion total views. They were also ranked #1 in nine out of eighteen years, dominating the period from the beginning of YouTube until 2017 (eclipsed for 2012-2013 by VICE, the overall #2 in the dataset), at which point there were four years in which Joe Rogan's channel occupied the #1 spot. It is telling that the reason that PowerfulJRE lost its throne was abdication: Rogan famously took his program exclusive to Spotify as part of a deal worth over $200 million. The most-viewed channel in 2022 was the Affiliated, right-wing Ben Shapiro.

There is somewhat more variation among the rest of the ranks, but as the relatively tight funnels in the top panels show, not *that* much more variation.

One of the limitations of this kind of macro-level analysis is the absence of any well-established "severe tests" to tell us when the system has shifted from dynamic stability to a more general flux. Replicating the graphs in Figure 12 for other year-to-year pairs generates more or less the same impression, with perhaps a bit more dispersion here, a bit less there.

One potentially useful test statistic is calculated based on the graph in the upper right: the absolute change in the rank of the top 100 channels. These top 4 percent of channels make up 49 percent of the total viewership, and restricting

Table 3 Degrees of dynamic stability

	Total Rank Change	Median Rank Change
2011	2720	19.5
2012	3002	14.5
2013	2953	16
2014	3050	14
2015	3785	17
2016	3200	14
2017	4721	25
2018	3406	17
2019	3896	19
2020	3448	16.5
2021	2654	14.5

the analysis to just this portion of the dataset allows me to calculate test statistics that are easily interpretable. Table 3 tracks both the total rank change and the median rank change by channel. The year listed is the beginning year, so the first row displays the rank change from 2010 to 2011 among the 100 most-viewed channels in 2010.

One limitation of this analysis is that it only includes channels that were active in each of the two years. That is, the explosion of a previously nonexisting channel into the top 100 would not affect these statistics; similarly, if a previously popular channel were to be banned, suspended, or voluntarily stop uploading videos/delete their account, this would not register much of a change. Hindman's theory suggests that these kinds of journey from nonexistence to the center of the attention economy should be rare, but as the case of Joe Rogan demonstrates, not impossible.

Caveats aside, Table 3 demonstrates a significant time trend: A staccato increase in the mobility of the system, peaking dramatically in 2016-2017 before returning to lower levels. Indeed, the final year in the analysis (2021–2022) saw the *lowest* total rank change in the entire time series, and very nearly the lowest median rank change as well.

Turning back to Figure 12 to compare to Figure 13, we can see the difference between the most stable year (2021) and the least stable year (2017). The increased dispersion is particularly visible in the top right panel, where the rises and falls in rank popularity among the top 100 channels are far more pronounced in 2017 than in 2021.

I did not begin this investigation with a specific reason to believe that this year was pivotal, so I can only speculate about the possible mechanisms. There

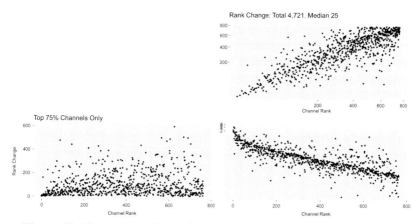

Figure 13 Change in rank (a), absolute rank change (b), absolute market share change (c). Change from 2016 to 2017. 1,018 channels included in analysis.

was certainly a lot going on around this time period: The largest increase in channel entry and rate of video uploading, especially among the right-wing Unaffiliated channels, was the period between 2016 and 2018. In previous work on a much narrower slice of the ecosystem, Phillips and I identified 2017 as the peak year for extreme right-wing content. While I tend to prefer an explanation based on Supply and Demand, the trace data are unable to disentangle this effect from a possible change in the recommendation algorithm or some other part of the platform infrastructure. In any event, this descriptive fact about the dynamic stability of the YouTube System is primarily an occasion for future research into the specific parameters that changed to cause this shakeup in popularity.

Overall, these results demonstrate continuity with research on other digital media ecosystems. The mechanisms of producer reputation and consumer habit are reinforced by platform affordances, but there is little evidence that the technology of YouTube is unique. The macro-level patterns of dynamic stability instead point towards a deep structure of attention online that also applies to the YouTube Apparatus.

10 The Academic Agenda for Studying Social Media

The theoretical contribution of the current manuscript takes an odd form. I have not proposed anything new, exactly; everything that I have done and everything that might be done with my work *could* already have been done. But the question of academic agenda setting is not primarily one of *theoretical capacity* but rather a decision over *practical trade-offs*: How should academics allocate our attention, our scarcest resource?

Given the impossible scale of YouTube and its importance in the political media ecosystem of the United States and beyond, I cannot seriously discuss, let alone rigorously estimate, all of the relevant parameters in the current manuscript. By sketching a larger and more realistic model, however, I hope to provide a framework by which the current analysis can be integrated with future contributions.

This approach – specifying the position of a given research project within a larger framework that aims at holistic understanding of complex phenomena – is my response to what has been called the "incoherency problem" of contemporary social science (Watts, 2017). That is, given the stakes of the topic under study, I agree with Watts' call for a more "solution-oriented" social science.

I am deeply nostalgic for the broadcast era, when the sociotechnical and regulatory environment enabled an economic system which in turn enabled an institutional arrangement that had the flexibility, the slack, and thus the *freedom* to create media that achieved a variety of aims, rather than being so tightly beholden to audience maximization. On YouTube, I have argued, the freedom of independent "Creators" is further diminished thanks to the expanded competition and pre-rationalized audience in the form of platform-created public measures.

Returning to the reflexive perspective with which I began, there are parallels with academic "media" production. Compared to for-profit daily media, academia is a unique institution; we are insulated from the harshest winds of market pressure and audience demands. To a much greater extent than other kinds of established institutional actors, over a 10 or 20 year time frame, *we get to decide what we study.*

But both "we" and "decide" are begging the relevant questions: Who is empowered to decide, using what decision-making institutions? Literally how do we set the academic agenda?

The traditional complaint about scholarly output is that it is too esoteric and insular, egghead professors creating elaborate castles in the air which no real humans will ever inhabit. More concretely, in my experience and in the Bennett and Iyengar (2008) critique, the problem is that the conservative institutional structure of academia allows powerful senior academics to replicate their theories through their grad students, with falsification never really on the table.

The dialectical response, especially felt in emerging and unsettled areas like digital politics, is a heavy emphasis on real-world policy impact and on scientific communication with the broader public. This has some important advantages over the previous model, but it has exposed us to many of the same pressures affecting the media. The more we search for "relevance," the further we descend the ivory tower, the more our incentives resemble those of the YouTubers seeking relatability with their audience – and the more accountable to nonacademics we become.

I am conflicted about my normative position here. With so much in flux, it is far from obvious that the ideal relationship between academics and society is the one we have inherited from the broadcast era. However, it is essential that we *acknowledge* these changes and think seriously and collectively about our goals and how best to achieve them. I believe that this will require major institutional reforms in academic training, career progression, and (most immediately) the structure of scholarly knowledge production. The only option that seems obviously unacceptable is the one I fear we are sleepwalking towards: changing as little as possible while the world changes around us.

There is an obvious tension, for example, between policy relevance for online politics and the *temporality* of traditional scholarship. The "industrial organization" of academia involves five-year (or longer) apprenticeships spent in intensive study of a narrow topic. How on earth is this supposed to work in the context of a rapidly-changing object of study? Consider TikTok. The platform has been available in the United States since late 2016; in early 2024, it looks possible that it will soon be banned. In this time period, it became one of the top three most-used social media platforms in the country.

Some digital politics may come and go faster than we could possibly study it; we can only speed up peer review so much without crippling the rigor that is central to our enterprise. So be it; all research has scope conditions. But ironically, YouTube is on the opposite end of the spectrum. As I have demonstrated, it has been one of the most stable and important platforms for American politics, with significant continuity with the political communication literature on previous media regimes. And yet the Element you have just read is the first comprehensive theoretical and quantitative treatment of YouTube Politics.

10.1 The Supply and Demand Framework

My primary theoretical intervention has been to argue that Demand creates its own Supply. Rather than focusing so much of our energy and attention on the pathway on the top of my motivating diagram, and particularly on the recommendation algorithm, I hope to motivate more attention to the reciprocal path of influence. The technical affordances of the YouTube System, combined with the asymmetric information and incentives facing the various actors, make a strong theoretical case for the importance of the influence of consumers on producers.

This combination of qualitative evidence about the experience of YouTubers and the extensive literature on media economics and audience theory motivated the empirical analysis in the previous section. A brief synthesis. First, the macro-scale results suggest that the marketplace of attention on YouTube behaves similarly to other digital media ecosystems. The dynamic stability over a fifteen-year time series, despite significant changes in the political environment, set of creators, and technological context, implies an upper bound on the influence of any one of those factors.

In other words, YouTube would still be a critical new technology and a locus for political discussion under a variety of different recommendation algorithms. This is why I think that both scholars and activists are better off thinking about YouTube from the lens of *Supply and Demand*.

But again, the economic metaphor only takes us so far. Money is the ultimate common denominator, and prices are an unparalleled information technology for facilitating market exchange. In contrast, the operators of the YouTube Apparatus process information intrinsic to the architecture of the YouTube System. This information is encoded into a variety of public measures which create distinct audiences with distinct effects on video producers.

Analytically, the classification of the dataset into institutionally-Affiliated channels and independent, Unaffiliated YouTubers provides empirical leverage on these effects. The further ideological categorization of the channels is not essential for my core argument, but it enables connection with the greater American political media ecosystem and will hopefully inform future research on YouTube Politics.

The trajectory of audiences created with simple viewership counts paints a story of the dominance of institutionally-Affiliated left-leaning media, in parallel with legacy American news media. The distinctly *YouTube* audience measures, however, involve a greater intensity of investment and engagement. Given the economic and social incentives facing independent YouTubers, I expected this audience to be more attracted to those channels. And indeed this is what I found, with the most pronounced effect for right-leaning channels beginning in the pivotal years of the 2016 US Presidential Campaign.

These findings, I argue, offer support for the Supply and Demand Framework. But this is a *framework*, not a specific *theory*. My theoretical goal is to inspire future researchers to develop these essential mid-level theories, in the hope of synthesizing a wealth of knowledge about each of the nodes and arrows in Figure 1. Again, this goal can only be achieved through changing how we set the academic agenda for studying YouTube.

This is all a bit abstract. How will this look in practice? The primary aim of political scientists is to understand effects on electoral democracy; in my Figure

1, this means a focus on "citizen beliefs." We have to begin with qualitative, thick description. For example, as Phillips and I wrote in our initial paper:

> Many people spend hours a day in contexts in which watching videos is simply easier than reading. Many people spend hours a day driving a truck or another vehicle, and they obviously cannot read while driving. The practice of white-collar workers performing their jobs while wearing headphones is increasingly accepted.

Kevin Roose's *New York Times* podcast "Rabbit Hole" makes an identical observation:

"And then when [Caleb, the interview subject] got his second job at the warehouse, they were actually allowed to listen to earphones – ... his YouTube watch time skyrockets even more. He's actually spending all day – from sunup to sundown – online."

The point is that we cannot understand YouTube Politics without understanding the larger sociotechnical context. YouTube allowed unprecedented growth in the production of audio/visual political media. People love videos; there are now videos about literally everything; and more people have the opportunity/and technological capacity to spend more of their time watching videos.

This is essential to understanding the political effect of YouTube. The algorithm is an efficient way to match supply and demand, and it certainly accelerates certain trends, but the crucial fact is that the demand is already there, created by a huge variety of factors exogenous to the videos uploaded to the platform.

There is still a role for political YouTubers to shape that demand, of course. Caleb's story makes it clear that he did not spring into the world fully formed as a xenophobic gun-and-religion-clutcher just waiting for someone to come along and "tell the truth about feminism" or whatever anti-woke issue was dominating the right-leaning YouTube Politics agenda at that moment; he was an alienated, lonely young man with a taste for alternative internet aesthetics. The people who made videos that spoke to people like him (due to structural social and economic factors) started off with a certain ideological bent. As information about Supply and Demand circulated around the whirlpool of the YouTube Apparatus, consumers and producers "radicalized" each other. There was no one steering this ship; the macro-political and technological tides had an impact, but not in a way that is straightforward to understand.

While I believe that my Framework (or something like it) gives necessary structure to the organization of scientific inquiry, our object of study here may well be too complex to ever be understood with the desired standard of rigor and precision. But policymakers, activists, and YouTubers are still going to *act*, and part of our aim should be to help them better align their intentions and the outcome of those actions.

As a qualitative example, Roose's podcast does an excellent job of exploring a mechanism behind what brought Caleb out of the far-right Rabbit Hole: more, better YouTube videos. Specifically, people like Destiny and Contrapoints who understand alternative internet aesthetics and make videos from a broadly left-wing perspective. Caleb watches some of their content and begins to see the flaws in his recently-developed far-right worldview.

The next step is to explore this proposed mechanism quantitatively, hope-fully with an experiment. But the intuition behind this anecdote informs my normative recommendation for how best to adapt to YouTube Politics. We are not going to be able to put the genie of social media – and particularly video-driven social media – back into the bottle. The success of democratic politics in the contemporary sociotechnical context requires meeting audiences where they are, producing media that appeals to their sensibilities while also advancing the political vision we want to see enacted in the world.

11 Self-Indulgent Postscript: Poetry as Social Science Methodology

The present media object encodes information as written text and statistical curves. As I have pointed out, this seems an ironic choice to explain a platform based on videos. But it is here, in the choice of *codes*, where the academic agenda is most inflexible.[5] We are axiomatically committed to the technol-ogy of reading and writing, supplemented in many cases by data analysis and visualization, as the medium in which we communicate.

In Section 3, I discussed the concept of *resonant metaphors* with reference to "echo chambers." I believe what follows is important, but it is admittedly far afield from the topic of YouTube, so I've waited until this postscript to explicate it.

"Methods" are taken to be techniques related to *data*. They can be qualitative, but in my experience methods have generally been quantitative. How are data coded? What statistical techniques have been applied to them? How are the results visualized?

"Methodology" is a field of research into these methods, aiming to improve them. The Society for Political Methodology and its flagship journal *Politi-cal Analysis* have come to define what "quantitative methods research" means

---

[5] With the possible exception of peer review – except that the latter is far more recent and con-tingent, and therefore I hope more malleable. I am optimistic that metascientific methodology will soon improve the process of peer review. At present, the process is deeply broken, at least for journal articles.

within the discipline of Political Science: a combination of applied statistics, programming code, and technical validation of data sources. Generally, "methodology" is a process by which these data operations are deemed to be "valid." The output of valid methods are combined with natural language to produce peer-reviewed manuscripts, like the current Element.

"Formal methods" are the exception that prove the rule: They do not make reference to any data. Instead, they combine natural language with another kind of language, generally some kind of applied mathematics, to produce their peer-reviewed manuscripts. "Formal methodology" involves validating novel combinations or neologisms within this formal language – it is thus a form of *formal poetry.*

In both cases, natural language serves as a bridge between the methods and the world. It must explain how the formal statistical, computational or mathematical operations help us understand politics. Only if *both* the methods and the natural language are "valid" does the manuscript succeed at communicating knowledge to the reader; the chain of knowledge production and transmission is only as strong as its weakest link.

The words and phrases that we use are therefore also *methods*. However, at present, we have paid very little attention to these methods; we have not developed a *poetic methodology.*

Consider "echo chambers." In the course of peer review for this manuscript, an anonymous reviewer contested my discussion of the topic in Section 3. My summary of the literature was that it finds that "echo chambers" don't exist– except among users in specialized (partisan or professional) networks. The reviewer wrote:

"Claims about the supposed lack of echo chambers online are also overstated here. Particularly with the release (finally!) of the Facebook 2020 studies, it's clear that most Facebook users, at least, are exposed overwhelmingly to like-minded content, even if the impact of that skewed exposure is extremely weak in terms of persuasion or polarization. I'd read much of the pre-existing literature as pointing to a similar conclusion: highly skewed exposure is well-established among us a substantial fraction of the public."

A poetic methodology would investigate the validity of the bridge between word and world; here, the question of whether "echo chamber" *means* "highly skewed exposure." The reviewer is advocating the mainstream position: that the "operationalization" of (the statistical operation corresponding to) the words "echo chamber" involves categorizing the ideological slant of media sources and measuring the aggregate media diet of citizens.

This strikes me as incorrect. Scholars of political communication have been analyzing the composition and ideological slant of media diets for as long as they have had the data and quantitative methods to do so, but without referring to even the most skewed media consumer as inhabiting an "echo chamber."

Bruns (2019) traces the history of the term, reminding us that the current usage dates to legal scholar Cass Sunstein's 2001 book *Republic.com* (the title is a considerably less successful metaphorical intervention). Bruns notes that Sunstein never provides a formal definition, let alone a quantitative operationalization, of his "echo chambers." But even if he had, it wouldn't be the final word; not even lawyers have the power to permanently fix semantic relationships.[6]

Bruns further establishes the slipperiness of the term, the way its definition has changed over time, as well as the fact that empirical evidence seems to have little impact on its popularity. The term "echo chamber," we might say, is low in "poetic validity" when it is operationalized by measuring the diversity of media diets.

But "echo chamber" is clearly a resonant metaphor. It captures *something* about the experience of using social media. To understand what this is, let's try a little phenomenology.

Close your eyes and imagine what it is like to physically *be in* an echo chamber, with other people inside. There is a cacophony of voices; they're distorted, and you can only pick out decontextualized snippets of conversation; you don't understand the acoustical properties that determine which voices you hear; it can sound like there are a whole host of voices even if there are only a few other speakers; if you yell over the din, you will hear your own voice reflected back at you.

Notably, if you really think about the experience, an "echo chamber" *has nothing whatsoever* to do with how it is most commonly operationalized. The "how biased is the media diet?" research question is a holdover from the broadcast era. In an era of constrained media supply and a fixed set of choices among linear broadcast or print technologies, this question makes sense. But it is exactly the wrong question to be asking in order to understand social media, in my opinion.

The experience of using social media is an *excellent* match for our phenomenological experiment, which I think is why the metaphor is so resonant. We could go even deeper, to the poetic reservoirs of the English language and the Greek myth of Echo and Narcissus. But I fear that might be a step too far for

---

[6] On the other hand, given that legal scholarship is analogous to social science except that natural language is the *only* code used to communicate, this field is likely to take poetic methodology more seriously, if not exactly in those terms.

even my most indulgent reader. So I'll let legendary political scientist V.O. Key lead the way (Key, 1966):

"The victorious candidate may regard his success as a vindication of his beliefs about why voters vote the way they do … This **narcissism** assumes its most repulsive form among election winners who have championed intolerance, who have stirred the passions and hatreds of people …

For a glaringly obvious reason … the voice of the people is but an **echo**. The output of an echo chamber bears an inevitable and invariable relationship to the input … the people's verdict can be no more than a selective reflection from among the alternatives and outlooks presented to them" (p2, emphasis mine).

The exact function of Key's "echo chamber" is different from that in our thought experiment: The "inevitable and invariable relationship" between output and input makes sense if the echo chamber is *empty*, and indeed this is how acoustic echo chambers are designed to work. This reflects the experience of elites and citizens of the 1960s, in which the latter had essentially zero capability to disseminate their beliefs and opinions. Politicians campaigned, and the people voted; the Big Three broadcast on television, and the people chose a channel to watch. The (incomplete but still dramatic) democratization of communicative capacity in the digital age has transformed the echo chamber from a static and finely tuned instrument into a constantly shifting cacophony.

Key's description of the causal chain of events follows exactly the same reciprocal relationship that is at the heart of the YouTube Apparatus:

"The perceptions of the behavior of the electorate held by political leaders, agitators and activists condition, if they do not fix, the types of appeals politicians employ as they seek popular support. These perceptions–or theories–affect the nature of the input to the echo chamber … and therefore control its output" (p6).

In order to understand the positions taken by the politicians who win office, their rhetorical appeals and strategic decisions, we have to begin with their *perceptions* of their audience. Key describes the progressive improvement and prominence of public opinion surveys and other tools of electorate measurement in the 1930s and 1950s, as well as the increasingly psychological theories of voter behavior, as playing a causal role in elite political decision-making. The "media" produced by politicians are their campaigns, among which the voters must ultimately decide.

The most important development, for the producers of both political media and political campaigns, is the technology by which they understand their audience. The "theories" that Key invokes extremely blunt; consider the "theory that the electorate was a pushover for a candidate who projected an appropriate 'father image'."

The explosion of quantitative data has qualitatively changed how campaigns perceive voters (Hersh, 2015). What were previously "theories" encoded in natural language have become data-visualized dashboards and statistical tables. Where once political orators spoke and heard their voice reflected, campaigns now use advanced sonar to map the echo chamber and run countless statistical simulations to predict the response to any utterance.

The crucial differences between presidential campaigns and political media are the temporality (once every four years vs daily and instantaneous) and the unique ontological status of the *vote*, a form of audience measurement with a fixed institutional connection to action. This produces the curious phenomenon of the burst of enthusiasm for Nate Silver-style election forecasting, followed soon after by disillusionment. The predictive accuracy of election forecasts is fundamentally limited by data; where other feedback loops have gotten dramatically faster, the electoral calendar retains its stubborn temporality.

The "narcissism" of the politician Key describes was made possible because they could only know their audience through the vote, and they were thus able to project their own greatness onto electoral success. In hindsight, this narcissism might not have been so bad; the confident leader who does what they think is right, regardless of whether it is possible, possesses a degree of narcissism.

In the present technosocial regime, for the operators of the YouTube Apparatus, this narcissism has been replaced by *nihilism*. There are indeed "echo chambers" on YouTube, but they are filled with an active and demanding audience. When the YouTuber uploads their video, whatever originality, creativity or *meaning* they intended to communicate is reduced to the public audience measures that the platform appends to the video. This quantification puts the video into immediate comparison with the YouTuber's previous videos, and indeed with every video on the platform.

It requires incredible willpower to ignore the reverberations of the ever-present audience on social media, to maintain an independent artistic vision or coherent ideological position. And for YouTubers attempting to make a living, the vast and intense competition makes it *impossible* to do so. The audience can simply click away if the YouTuber displeases them. The pressure of having millions of bosses issuing conflicting demands can produce "Creator burnout" or worse.

My poetic aspiration is that whenever you read the words "YouTube Creator" you think instead of "Audience Creation." Social media does not create powerful Influencers but rather powerless marionettes, dancing jerkily to quantified audience tugs.

I have emphasized this direction of influence because I think that it is dramatically under-appreciated. Our intuitions about media effects have a hangover from the broadcast era. But it is of course inaccurate to posit any unmoved movers in the social world, and in reality the influence is reciprocal. Neither the operators of the YouTube Apparatus nor the platform itself are unchanged as the cycle of production and consumption spins.

The direction of influence is circular, but each pass around the circle does not return us to the same place. Flusser says that "this circularity is not of a wheel but of a whirlpool." The frenzied production and consumption of political media within the YouTube Apparatus does not make any *progress* in the sense of developing ideological agendas (*destinations*) or creating social movements (*capacity*). Instead, the whirlpool drags everything down into itself.

Flusser summarizes the present situation:

"The better the apparatus works, the more autonomous of independent opinion and decision it becomes, and the feedback between [media] and public opinion reinforces its ever-more-automatic programming. The tendency appears to be in the direction of a ... mass society within which life will become ever lonelier and more senseless."

This is what I mean by *nihilism*: Communication within the YouTube Apparatus *has no meaning*. This is easiest to see in the emergence of bizarre video genres which have emerged from the whirlpool: the mukbang, in which the YouTuber consumes massive quantities of food; ASMR, in which the YouTuber makes crinkling whispering sounds distorted by their digital microphone. And recall the horrific videos of Peppa Pig eating her father or drinking bleach from Section 3.

The same fundamental process is taking place with YouTube Politics. The social and political world continues to produce events to be fed into the Apparatus, which transforms them into a meaningless cycle of videos and reactions. There is no one steering the ship, so it doesn't go anywhere but down. Compared to the politics of the past, particularly before the middle of the 20th century, the nihilism of the YouTube Apparatus is intensely de-politicizing.

I'll give the last word to Key, whose work proves remarkably prescient:

"Over the longer run the properties of the echo chamber itself may themselves be altered. Fed a steady diet of buncombe, the people may come to expect and to respond with highest probability to buncombe. And those leaders most skilled in the propagation of buncombe may gain lasting advantage in the recurring struggles for popular favor." (p7)

Buncombe in, buncombe out. Echo chamber or whirlpool, our political media environment cannot succeed unless both producers and consumers are committed to communicating *meaning* rather than treating communication as merely a functional means to an end.

References

Allen, Jennifer, Baird Howland, Markus Mobius, David Rothschild, and Duncan J Watts. 2020. "Evaluating the fake news problem at the scale of the information ecosystem." *Science Advances* 6 (14): eaay3539.

Arceneaux, Kevin, Timothy B Gravelle, Mathias Osmundsen, et al. 2021. "Some people just want to watch the world burn: The prevalence, psychology and politics of the 'Need for Chaos'." *Philosophical Transactions of the Royal Society B* 376 (1822): 20200147.

Archer, Allison M, and Joshua Clinton. 2018. "Changing owners, changing content: Does who owns the news matter for the news?" *Political Communication* 35 (3): 353–370.

Askonas, Jon. 2022. "How Stewart made tucker." *The New Atlantis* (69): 3–35.

Barberá, Pablo, Andreu Casas, Jonathan Nagler, et al. 2019. "Who leads? Who follows? Measuring issue attention and agenda setting by legislators and the mass public using social media data." *American Political Science Review* 113 (4): 883–901.

Beniger, James. 2009. *The control revolution: Technological and economic origins of the information society*. Harvard University Press.

Bennett, W Lance, and Shanto Iyengar. 2008. "A new era of minimal effects? The changing foundations of political communication." *Journal of Communication* 58 (4): 707–731.

Bisbee, James, Jennifer Larson, and Kevin Munger. 2022. "# polisci Twitter: A descriptive analysis of how political scientists use Twitter in 2019." *Perspectives on Politics* 20 (3): 879–900.

Bode, Leticia, and Emily K Vraga. 2015. "In related news, that was wrong: The correction of misinformation through related stories functionality in social media." *Journal of Communication* 65 (4): 619–638.

Boydstun, Amber E. 2013. *Making the news: Politics, the media, and agenda setting*. University of Chicago Press.

Boydstun, Amber E, Anne Hardy, and Stefaan Walgrave. 2014. "Two faces of media attention: Media storm versus non-storm coverage." *Political Communication* 31 (4): 509–531.

Bridle, James. 2017. "Something is wrong on the internet." *Medium. https:// medium.com/@jamesbridle/something-is-wrong-on-the-internet-c39c4712 71d2 [consultado 22/11/2017]* .

Brown, Megan A, James Bisbee, Angela Lai, et al. 2022. "Echo chambers, rabbit holes, and algorithmic bias: How YouTube recommends content to real users." *SSRN 4114905.*

Bruns, Axel. 2019. "It's not the technology, stupid: How the 'Echo Chamber'and 'Filter Bubble' metaphors have failed us." *International Association for Media and Communication Research.*

Buntain, Cody, Richard Bonneau, Jonathan Nagler, and Joshua A Tucker. 2021. "YouTube recommendations and effects on sharing across online social platforms." *Proceedings of the ACM on Human-Computer Interaction* 5 (CSCW1): 1–26.

Carlson, Matt. 2017. *Journalistic authority: Legitimating news in the digital era.* Columbia University Press.

Chadwick, Andrew. 2017. *The hybrid media system: Politics and power.* Oxford University Press.

Chaffee, Steven H, and Miriam J Metzger. 2001. "The end of mass communication?" *Mass Communication & Society* 4 (4): 365–379.

Christin, Angèle. 2020. *Metrics at work: Journalism and the contested meaning of algorithms.* Princeton University Press.

Christin, Angèle, and Rebecca Lewis. 2021. "The drama of metrics: Status, spectacle, and resistance among YouTube drama creators." *Social Media+ Society* 7 (1): 2056305121999660.

Converse, Phillip. 1964. "The nature of belief systems in mass publics. In *Ideology and discontent*, ed. David Apter. Free Press, pp. 56–89."

Cook, John, Ullrich Ecker, and Stephan Lewandowsky. 2015. "Misinformation and how to correct it." *Emerging Trends in the Social and Behavioral Sciences: An Interdisciplinary, Searchable, and Linkable Resource* pp. 1–17.

Coppock, Alexander. 2021. "Persuasion in parallel." *Chicago Studies in American Politics.*

Cowen, Tyler. 2018. "Eric Schmidt on the life-changing magic of systematizing, scaling, and saying 'Thanks'." *Medium. https://medium.com/conversa tions-with-tyler/eric-schmidt-tyler-cowen-google-ec33aa3e6dae.*

DellaPosta, Daniel. 2020. "Pluralistic collapse: The 'oil spill' model of mass opinion polarization." *American Sociological Review* 85 (3): 507–536.

DellaPosta, Daniel, Yongren Shi, and Michael Macy. 2015. "Why do liberals drink lattes?" *American Journal of Sociology* 120 (5): 1473–1511.

Deutsch, Karl W. 1963. The nerves of government; models of political communication and control. *Technical Report.*

Feyerabend, Paul K. 1975. "Against method: Outline of an anarchistic theory of knowledge." Verso Books.

Flusser, Vilém. 2022. *Communicology: Mutations in human relations?* Stanford University Press.

Freelon, Deen, Meredith L Pruden, and Daniel Malmer. 2023. "# political-communicationsowhite: Race and politics in nine communication journals, 1991–2021." *Political Communication* 40 (4):1–19.

Garrett, R Kelly, and Brian E Weeks. 2013. "The promise and peril of real-time corrections to political misperceptions". In *Proceedings of the 2013 conference on computer supported cooperative work*. ACM pp. 1047–1058.

Gentzkow, Matthew, and Jesse M Shapiro. 2006. "Media bias and reputation." *Journal of political Economy* 114 (2): 280–316.

Gentzkow, Matthew, and Jesse M Shapiro. 2008. "Competition and truth in the market for news." *The Journal of Economic Perspectives* 22 (2): 133–154.

Gentzkow, Matthew, and Jesse M Shapiro. 2010. "What drives media slant? Evidence from US daily newspapers." *Econometrica* 78 (1): 35–71.

Gerring, John. 2012. "Mere description." *British Journal of Political Science* 42 (4): 721–746.

Giddens, Anthony. 1986. *The constitution of society: Outline of the theory of structuration*. Vol. 349. University of California Press.

Guess, Andrew, and Alexander Coppock. 2020. "Does counter-attitudinal information cause backlash? Results from three large survey experiments." *British Journal of Political Science* 50 (4): 1497–1515.

Guess, Andrew M. 2021. "(Almost) Everything in moderation: New evidence on Americans' online media diets." *American Journal of Political Science* 65 (4): 1007–1022.

Gurri, Martin. 2018. *The revolt of the public and the crisis of authority in the new millennium*. Stripe Press.

Hamilton, James. 2004. *All the news that's fit to sell: How the market transforms information into news*. Princeton University Press.

Hamilton, James. 2016. *Democracy's detectives*. Harvard University Press.

Hersh, Eitan D. 2015. *Hacking the electorate: How campaigns perceive voters*. Cambridge University Press.

Hindman, Matthew. 2008. *The myth of digital democracy*. Princeton University Press.

Hindman, Matthew. 2018. *The internet trap: How the digital economy builds monopolies and undermines democracy*. Princeton University Press.

Hofstadter, Richard. 2012. *The paranoid style in American politics*. Vintage.

Hosseinmardi, Homa, Amir Ghasemian, Aaron Clauset, et al. 2020. "Evaluating the scale, growth, and origins of right-wing echo chambers on YouTube." *arXiv preprint arXiv:2011.12843*.

Jenkins, Henry, Sam Ford, and Joshua Green. 2013. "Spreadable media: Creating value and meaning in a networked culture." New York University Press.

Kaplan, Richard. 2009. "The origins of objectivity in American journalism." In Stuart Allan, ed., *The Routledge companion to news and journalism*. Routledge, pp. 69–81.

Karpf, David. 2019. "On digital disinformation and democratic myths." *Mediawell, Social Science Research Council* 10.

Kata, Anna. 2010. "A postmodern Pandora's box: Anti-vaccination misinformation on the Internet." *Vaccine* 28 (7): 1709–1716.

Kata, Anna. 2012. "Anti-vaccine activists, Web 2.0, and the postmodern paradigm–An overview of tactics and tropes used online by the anti-vaccination movement." *Vaccine* 30 (25): 3778–3789.

Katz, Elihu, and Paul Felix Lazarsfeld. 1964. *Personal influence, The part played by people in the flow of mass communications*. Transaction.

Key, Valdimer Orlando. 1966. *The responsible electorate: Rationality in presidential voting 1936–1960*. Harvard University Press.

Klar, Samara, and Yanna Krupnikov. 2016. *Independent politics*. Cambridge University Press.

Ladd, Jonathan M. 2011. *Why Americans hate the media and how it matters*. Princeton University Press.

Lai, Angela, Megan A Brown, James Bisbee, et al. 2022. "Estimating the ideology of political YouTube videos." *SSRN*.

Lasswell, Harold D. 1927. *Propaganda technique in the world war*. Ravenio Books.

Latour, Bruno, and Steve Woolgar. 2013. *Laboratory life: The construction of scientific facts*. Princeton University Press.

Ledwich, Mark, and Anna Zaitsev. 2020. "Algorithmic extremism: Examining YouTube's rabbit hole of radicalization." *First Monday* 25 (3).

Ledwich, Mark, Anna Zaitsev, and Anton Laukemper. 2022. "Radical bubbles on YouTube? Revisiting algorithmic extremism with personalised recommendations." *First Monday* 27 (12).

Lewis, Rebecca. 2018. "Alternative influence: Broadcasting the reactionary right on YouTube." *Data & Society* .

Lewis, Rebecca. 2020. " 'This is what the news won't show you': YouTube Creators and the Reactionary Politics of Micro-celebrity." *Television & New Media* 21 (2): 201–217.

Martin, Gregory J, and Joshua McCrain. 2019. "Local news and national politics." *American Political Science Review* 113 (2): 372–384.

Merkley, Eric. 2020. "Anti-intellectualism, populism, and motivated resistance to expert consensus." *Public Opinion Quarterly* 84 (1): 24–48.

Mider, Zachary. 2016. "What kind of man spends millions to elect Ted Cruz?" *Bloomberg Politics*.

Munger, Kevin. 2019. "The limited value of non-replicable field experiments in contexts with low temporal validity." *Social Media+ Society* 5 (3): 2056305119859294.

Munger, Kevin. 2020. "All the news that's fit to click: The economics of clickbait media." *Political Communication* 37 (3): 376–397.

Munger, Kevin, Andrew M Guess, and Eszter Hargittai. 2021. "Quantitative description of digital media: A modest proposal to disrupt academic publishing." *Journal of Quantitative Description: Digital Media* 1, pp. 1–13.

Munger, Kevin, and Joseph Phillips. 2022. "Right-wing YouTube: A supply and demand perspective." *International Journal of Press/Politics* 27 (1): 186–219.

Mutz, Diana C. 1998. *Impersonal influence: How perceptions of mass collectives affect political attitudes*. Cambridge University Press.

Napoli, Philip M. 2011. *Audience evolution: New technologies and the transformation of media audiences*. Columbia University Press.

Napoli, Philip M. 2019. *Social media and the public interest: Media regulation in the disinformation age*. Columbia University Press.

Nelson, Jacob L, and James G Webster. 2016. "Audience currencies in the age of big data." *International Journal on Media Management* 18 (1): 9–24.

O'Callaghan, Derek, Derek Greene, Maura Conway, Joe Carthy, and Pádraig Cunningham. 2015. "Down the (white) rabbit hole: The extreme right and online recommender systems." *Social Science Computer Review* 33 (4): 459–478.

Pearl, Judea. 1995. "Causal diagrams for empirical research." *Biometrika* 82 (4): 669–688.

Perrin, Andrew, and Monica Anderson. 2019. *Social media use in 2019*. Pew.

Philips, Whitney, and Ryan Milner. 2020. *You are here: A field guide for navigating polluted information*. MIT Press.

Postman, Neil. 2005. *Amusing ourselves to death: Public discourse in the age of show business*. Penguin.

Ribeiro, Manoel H, Raphael Ottoni, Robert West, Virgílio A. F. Almeida, and Wagner Meira Jr. 2020. Auditing radicalization pathways on YouTube. In *Proceedings of the 2020 Conference on Fairness, Accountability, and Transparency*. pp. 131–141.

Roose, Kevin. 2019. "The making of a YouTube radical." *The New York Times*. *www.nytimes.com/interactive/2019/06/08/technology/youtuberadical.html*.

Simon, Felix M, and Chico Q Camargo. 2023. "Autopsy of a metaphor: The origins, use and blind spots of the 'infodemic'." *New Media & Society* 25 (8): 2219–2240.

Soroka, Stuart N, and Christopher Wlezien. 2010. *Degrees of democracy: Politics, public opinion, and policy*. Cambridge University Press.

Soroka, Stuart N, and Christopher Wlezien. 2022. *Information and democracy*. Cambridge University Press.

Starr, Paul. 2004. "The creation of the media: Political origins of modern communications." New York: Basic Books.

Stocking, Galen, Patrick Van Kessel, Michael Barthel, Katerina Eva Matsa, and Maya Khuzam. 2020. "Many Americans get news on YouTube, where news organizations and independent producers thrive side by side." *Pew Research Center* .

Stroud, Natalie Jomini. 2017. "Selective exposure theories." In Kenski, Kate, and Kathleen Hall Jamieson, eds., *The Oxford handbook of political communication*, pp. 531–548.

Tufekci, Zeynep. 2018. "YouTube, the great radicalizer." *The New York Times* 12: 15.

Uscinski, Joseph E, Adam M Enders, Michelle I Seelig, et al. 2021. "American politics in two dimensions: partisan and ideological identities versus anti-establishment orientations." *American Journal of Political Science* 65 (4): 877–895.

Usher, Nikki. 2014. *Making news at the New York times*. University of Michigan Press.

Walker, Mason, and Katerina Eva Matsa. 2021. *News consumption across social media in 2021*. Pew.

Watts, Duncan J. 2017. "Should social science be more solution-oriented?" *Nature Human Behaviour* 1 (1): 1–5.

Webster, James G. 2011. "The duality of media: A structurational theory of public attention." *Communication Theory* 21 (1): 43–66.

Webster, James G. 2014. *The marketplace of attention: How audiences take shape in a digital age*. MIT Press.

Weiss, Bari. 2020. "Did I just get yanged?" *The New York Times*. *www.nytimes .com/2020/01/30/opinion/sunday/andrew-yang-2020.html*.

Williams, Bruce A, and Michael X Delli Carpini. 2011. *After broadcast news: Media regimes, democracy, and the new information environment.* Cambridge University Press.

Wlezien, Christopher. 1995. "The public as thermostat: Dynamics of preferences for spending." *American Journal of Political Science* 39 (4): 981–1000.

Wlezien, Christopher. 2023. "News and public opinion: Which comes first?" *Journal of Politics* 86 (1): 1–17.

Cambridge Elements ☰

Politics and Communication

Stuart Soroka
University of California

Stuart Soroka is a Professor in the Department of Communication at the University of California, Los Angeles, and Adjunct Research Professor at the Center for Political Studies at the Institute for Social Research, University of Michigan. His research focuses on political communication, political psychology, and the relationships between public policy, public opinion, and mass media. His books with Cambridge University Press include The Increasing Viability of Good News (2021, with Yanna Krupnikov), Negativity in Democratic Politics (2014), Information and Democracy (forthcoming, with Christopher Wlezien) and Degrees of Democracy (2010, with Christopher Wlezien).

About the series

Cambridge Elements in Politics and Communication publishes research focused on the intersection of media, technology, and politics. The series emphasizes forward-looking reviews of the field, path-breaking theoretical and methodological innovations, and the timely application of social-scientific theory and methods to current developments in politics and communication around the world.

Cambridge Elements ≡

Politics and Communication

Printed in the United States
by Baker & Taylor Publisher Services